THE SOUTHERN
GOSPEL MUSIC
COOKBOOK

THE SOUTHERN GOSPEL MUSIC COOKBOOK

*Favorite Recipes from
More Than 100 Gospel Music
Performers*

BETHNI HEMPHILL, BRENDA MCCLAIN,
KEN BECK, AND JIM CLARK

CUMBERLAND HOUSE PUBLISHING

Nashville, Tennessee

Published by Cumberland House Publishing, Inc., 431 Harding Industrial Drive, Nashville, Tennessee37211-3160.

Design by Bruce Gore, Gore Studios, Inc.

Library of Congress Cataloging-in-Publication Data

The southern gospel music cookbook : favorite recipes from more than 100 gospel music performers / Bethni Hemphill . . . [et al.].
    p.   cm.
   Includes index.
   ISBN 1–888952–76–8 (pbk.)
   1. Cookery. 2. Gospel musicians—Miscellanea. 3. Gospel music—Miscellanea. I. Hemphill, Bethni, 1964—
TX714.S625   1998
641.5—dc21   98–5844
                                     CIP

Printed in the United States of America
1 2 3 4 5 6 7 8 — 01 00 99 98

CONTENTS

"BLESSED ARE THOSE WHO
HUNGER AND THIRST FOR RIGHTEOUSNESS,
FOR THEY SHALL BE FILLED."

—*Matthew 5:6*

All things are ready,
Come to the feast,
Come for the table now is spread.
Ye famishing, ye weary come,
And thou shalt be richly fed.

Hear the invitation,
Come whosoever will.
Praise God for full salvation,
For whosover will.

—*Charlotte G. Homer*
   and W. A. Ogden

ACKNOWLEDGMENTS

THIS BOOK would not have been possible without a lot of help and encouragement and good thoughts and prayers from many people. In addition to all of the gospel music artists and their families who generously shared the recipes that you'll enjoy throughout this book, we wish to thank others who helped us gather recipes, photographs, and information.

We thank Clarke Beasley, Jerry and Carolyn Kirksey, Ken Kirksey, Rick Francis, Jamie Tedder, Heather Campbell, Jo Harper, Ed Harper and Harper & Associates, Lance LeRoy, Danny Jones, Norman Holland, Celeste Winstead and Daywind Records, Brian Covert, Bob Terrell, Jackie Leach, April Potter, Stacey Scheirer, Pam Slaney, Mr. and Mrs. Les Beasley, Pamela Stansberry, T. Clarke Miller, Peg McKamey Bean, Dixie McKeithen, Beckie Simmons, Brandon Abbott and Homeland Records, Rodney Hatfield and Spring Hill Records, Dottie Bunn, Randall Franks, Kathy Harris, Judith Blatchford, Greystone Communications, Paul Heil and The Southern Gospel Music Guild, Judy Murata, and The National Quartet Convention.

We especially wish to acknowledge assistance from *The Singing News* for allowing us to use some recipes of gospel artists that the magazine has collected over the years. We're also grateful to *The Singing News, The Gospel Voice Magazine,* Rick Francis, and *The Music City News* for their archival work and help in locating vintage photographs of several groups.

We thank Publisher Ron Pitkin at Cumberland House for believing in this project. For helping turn our raw ingredients into a finished product, we express our appreciation to editor Julie Pitkin and to Lori McNeese. And for helping make it possible that you could actually hear about and find this book, we thank vice president of marketing and sales Julie Jayne.

We also appreciate the support and patience of our families as we worked on this project. Bethni wishes to thank her husband Trent and their children, Madeleine and William. Brenda thanks her mother, Josie Dee Reynolds McClain, and her sisters, Marion Leigh Greene, Dee Ann Howell, and Odean Floyd Reynolds, Joy Hooper, and Marion Burnquist, who have always cooked so I haven't had to. Ken thanks his wife Wendy, daughter Kylie, and son Cole. Jim wishes to thank his wife, Mary.

Thanks to all who helped us with your good thoughts and hard work!

INTRODUCTION

SOUTHERN GOSPEL music and good home-cooked food have gone hand in hand since that first all-day singing or week-long brush arbor meeting way back in the 1800s.

Anyone who has grown up in the rural South can attest to the incredible dinner-on-the-ground meals that have left men, women, boys, and girls holding their sides and groaning in delicious agony after one of these sumptuous repasts.

Bob Terrell describes a typical scene from one of these feasts at an all-day singing in his book *The Music Men:*

"At noon, after a couple of hours of preliminary singing, the convention broke for dinner-on-the-ground, during which the ladies of the community showed off their culinary skills, weighting long tables in the churchyard with bowls and platters of country ham, fried chicken, roast beef, peas, beans, corn, banana pudding, fried apple and peach pies, baked pies and cakes of every flavor, and jugs of iced tea, lemonade, and coffee."

Umm, umm, brings back wonderful memories, not to mention making you hungry, doesn't it?

While the taste of good food hasn't changed, Southern Gospel music has. Yet it may be one of the best-kept secrets in the United States. Just about every weekend of the year, nearly two hundred Southern Gospel quartets perform at concert arenas, major auditoriums, theme parks, and churches across the country—drawing thousands of fans.

With *The Southern Gospel Cookbook*, we have gone to those who know the music best—those who write the songs and sing them—and have gathered from them some of their all-time favorite recipes. This collection contains over two hundred recipes from more than one hundred groups and artists. Most of the recipes are connected to a Southern raising, with many having been handed down through families for generations.

There are breads and biscuits, libations and salads, beef, fowl, and fish as well as sweet meats and sweet treats. There's no doubt about it: professional gospel musicians know good food. Those long hours on the road, and late-night meals at truck stops have taught the singers and musicians the value of an enjoyable meal.

We've tried to capture some of the history of Southern Gospel in these pages with plenty of photographs, current and vintage, that you will enjoy as well as a few short stories, fascinating tidbits, and some fun-filled quizzes to test your knowledge of the genre that is one of America's fastest-growing in popularity.

So, start turning the pages and check out some mouth-watering recipes along with some precious memories of those who bring us this beloved music.

And once you spot a recipe you think will awaken your taste buds, head for the kitchen and get to cooking. If you like it as much as we think you will, be sure and share it with a neighbor. There's nothing that goes better with good food than good company.

B.H., B.M., K.B., and J.C.

The Gospel Singing Caravan Chorus, shown here in 1964, was formed in late 1961 and featured four gospel groups in what was to become, behind The Gospel Singing Jubilee, *the second most popular gospel music television show* The Gospel Caravan. *The Caravan consisted of The LeFevres of Atlanta ("America's most versatile singers"), The Blue Ridge Quartet of Spartanburg, South Carolina ("the sweetest singing this side of heaven"), The Johnson Sisters of Birmingham, Alabama ("Sweethearts of gospel music"), and The Prophets of Knoxville, Tennessee ("the most unique sound in gospel music").*

The late Wally Fowler was a singer, writer and pioneer. He owned and operated the original Oak Ridge Boys Quartet, wrote hundreds of songs, including Eddy Arnold's first million-seller, "That's How Much I Love You, Baby." In the Southern Gospel world he'll go down in history as the originator of the All-Night Gospel Sing.

A BRIEF HISTORY OF SOUTHERN GOSPEL MUSIC

THE POPULARITY of Southern Gospel music today can be traced back to the days of the Pilgrims with their hymns and to the African Americans singing spirituals, as gospel music comes from the roots of America and the Christian faith.

Southern Gospel music made its first impact in popular entertainment around 1910 when professional quartets performed both popular tunes and gospel songs in public appearances. Those early professional gospel pioneers sang by reading notes which were shaped in geometrical figures; round, triangular, square, flag-shaped, bowl-shaped and called Do, Re, Mi, Fa, So, La, Ti, Do.

In the late 1920s, the gospel quartets hit full stride as they sang songs about the love of God and of better times ahead. It was a sound and message that deprived, Depression-era Americans were starving for. But the good music outlived the dark times of the Depression.

These male quarterts were filled by a first or high tenor, a lead singer or second tenor, a baritone, and a bass singer. They performed strictly as the music led them. Only later in the 1950s, did the singers begin swapping parts, an idea sprung by pianist Jackie Marshall, who accompanied The Blackwood Brothers.

But that first era of Southern Gospel music borrows its success from men who simply wanted to peddle as many songbooks as possible. One of those primarily responsible for developing and popularizing gospel music was James D. Vaughan.

Up until about 1870, Southern sacred songbooks were written in a four-note system, commonly referred to as "Sacred Harp." The Virginia publishing company of Ruebush/Kiefer issued a new book with songs written on a seven-note scale. The publishers released a new publication each month and, to help promote sales, they started a singing school. The school taught songs with the shaped notes over the more official and proper round ones.

Vaughan attended a Ruebush/Kiefer School and learned this style of reading music and in 1902 opened his own James D. Vaughan Publishing Company. It was Vaughan who hit upon the idea of sending gospel quartets on the road to promote his songbooks. So in May of 1910, The Vaughan Quartet hit the trail as the first Southern Gospel quartet and true pioneers of their musical genre.

That year Vaughan's book sales doubled to sixty thousand and the business continued to thrive. In 1911 he opened a Vaughan School of Music in Lawrenceburg, Tenn., where many youngsters learned to sing and perform from men who thought of themselves not so much as gospel singers as simply music men.

By 1921 Vaughan was making phonograph records, advertised as "the first and only Southern records to be placed on the market." The first gospel quartet record ever made was "I Couldn't Hear Nobody Pray," by The Vaughan Quartet consisting of

Hillman Barnard, Kieffer Vaughan, Walter B. Seale, and Ray Collins.

On November 21, 1922, Vaughan took a giant step further by getting his music on the airwaves via his WOAN radio station, the first radio station in Tennessee. Calling his company the James D. Vaughan Radiophone Broadcasting Station, the music man aired night broadcasts from 1921 to 1929. The shows were extraordinarily popular and featured quartets, solos, duets, trios, and orchestras.

Throughout the 1920s, the Vaughan Music Company was a prominent force in gospel music from the Southern East Coast to as far west as New Mexico and as far north as the Mason-Dixon Line. And Vaughan, who wrote more than five hundred songs himself, established Vaughan Schools of Music across the country.

In the meantime, disciples of Vaughan branched into the gospel music publishing business themselves — most prominently, V.O. Stamps and J.R. Baxter Jr. These popular quartets, especially the radio quartets, made rural kids of the 1930s long to become singers. But business slowed down as the Depression kept folks cash-poor and cut songbook sales in half for all publishers and made it impossible for any quartet to make a living simply by singing.

One of Vaughan's competitors, the Stamps School of Music, proved stable enough to survive the Depresssion and flourished up into the 1950s. Stamps Schools taught quartet singing and piano-playing to thousands upon thousands of kids. From these schools came hundreds of men and women who went into professional gospel singing.

During the pre-World War II era, singing conventions became a community-wide, popular form of entertainment. They were all-day affairs that drew young and old alike, usually to churchhouses or schoolhouses.

But the advent of World War II closed the professional gospel singing industry as gasoline was rationed and many materials, such as rubber, were banned to the public and reserved only for military use. With no fuel or wheels, the quartets stayed at home.

In the late 1940s, a new day dawned for those who loved songs of praise and hymns. The modern era of Southern Gospel was ushered in by Wally Fowler with his first All-Night Singing in Nashville's Ryman Auditorim on November 5, 1948.

That first Wally Fowler's Gospel and Spiritual All-Night Singing, as it was billed, included a lineup of Wally Fowler and the Oak Ridge Quartet, Frank Stamps and the Stamps Quartet, The Stamps All-Star Quartet, The Blackwood Brothers Quartet, G.E. Vaughan and the Vaughan Radio Quartet, Deacon Utley and the Smile-A-While Quartet, The Speer Family, Milton Estes and The Musical Millers Quartet, The Gospelaires Quartet, and The Sunshine Boys.

This all-night affair was a spectacular success, not to mention a sellout, and gave birth to all-night singings across the South, as quartets left the schoolhouses and church buildings and rented auditoriums to perform before packed venues. With as many as a half dozen quartets performing, tickets sold much more easily than if just one or two acts were playing.

Many churches still held all-day singings with dinner on the ground, but at many of the singing conventions, the professional groups were still being paid by the passing-of-the-hat method, and most singers barely broke even at that.

In the meantime, the popular Blackwood Brothers and The Statesmen began teaming for concert dates and were easily the two most powerful groups in the business of gospel music throughout the 1950s.

Many singers longed to follow in their musical shoes. Especially in hotbeds of quartet singing in Florida, Texas, Tennessee, Alabama, Georgia, and North Carolina, great singers and great quartets sprang forth.

As the all-night singings changed the face of the business, more groups tried to get into the business. Around 1955, the market got tough—possibly from too many groups drinking from the same trough. The acts became more entertainment-orientated, compared to the more serious spirituality of gospel musicians today. A slump began.

Jack Clark of The Homeland Harmony Quartet and The Harvesters Quartet, recalled that "the quartet business was good in the late forties and early fifties, but the entire nation wasn't ready for it. The business became so good that suddenly everybody had a gospel quartet trying to book dates, and there were just not enough dates to go around. As a result, a lot of quartet people had to go back to doing something else. The business became overpopulated and had to go through a weeding out process. The ones who were really good, really dedicated, and took care of their business, survived. The rest fell by the wayside. After that and only after that, was when the real growth in the gospel quartet business began to take place, and there has been a pretty steady growth since."

The end of the era of gospel music as pure Christian entertainment came with the breakup of the Statesmen-Blackwood Brothers team. Up to this point, in the mid-1960s, Southern Gospel had been four men standing around a piano singing.

Various groups tried to do things differently and television played a hand as the golden era of gospel quartets melted away and the modern era of mostly mixed groups with more salvation songs came in.

"The biggest impact and change and growth was when we got *The Singing Jubilee,*" says Southern Gospel journalist and *Singing*

News editor Jerry Kirksey. "The show was spun off of the successful *Gospel Songshop* and was an hourlong color show with The Florida Boys in 1964. In its peak, it played in every major television market in the country." It increased the popularity of Southern Gospel music and got exposure for The Happy Goodman Family, The Dixie Echoes, The Couriers, and The Florida Boys, the host group.

Those four groups carried the show for its first four seasons. Later a variety of groups came on: The Hemphills and The Inspirations, among others, in the late 1960s. "Many of these groups were were not the traditional four men singing four-part harmony, but presented a totally different style. The show gave those styles lots of exposure."

Besides television, the other major factor that changed the face of Southern Gospel was the coming of the artist development labels in the late 1970s and early 1980s. Previously an act had to be a big-time artist to be signed to a major label, and in Southern Gospel there were mainly two, Canaan and Heartwarming Records.

"Ronnie Drake in Nashville created a label, Windchimes," Kirksey recalls. "His concept was to take an artist that was good but that nobody had ever heard of and put out a single and promote that record to radio stations.

"As the industry grew to be patterned after secular music, it became that you could get a hit song and create an 'overnight' artist. Drake saw that we *(The Singing News)* had charts, and if he could get a hit song, he had a hit artist. So we went from a group-driven industry to a song-driven industry. Before you had to be a Blackwoods or Statesmen or The Florida Boys to get a hit song."

So Drake broke new ground with the group HeavenBound and their hit song "Canaan's Land is Just in Sight." By radio promotion, the song became a big hit, and the group became much in demand.

So, the face of Southen Gospel was changed anew as artist development labels brought in a huge variety of new talent and the results were an influx of younger, popular groups. These acts included solo artists, duets, trios, mixed quartets, and even bluegrass gospel acts and acts that were almost comtemporary Christian musicians in nature. There were some repercussions from the traditional groups, but the results were good for all as each one of the new styles brought in new fans.

Most recently, the innovations of Bill Gaither have turned Southern Gospel into an even more popular form of entertainment. In the mid-1990s, Gaither began making Southern Gospel videos, which sold into the millions and led to cable television specials on The Nashville Network, TBN, ACTS, and the Family Channel.

The television shows have not only popularized up-and-coming groups, but have recreated careers for artists who had retired. The shows have an impact, not just in the United States, but to Europe as well. "It's kind of an explosion," is how Kirksey sums up the genre in the late 1990s.

"There were 124,000 concerts in 1996, and 36 million fans attended those concerts. There are 106 groups doing 106 concerts every Thursday through Sunday night," he says. But that's not all. There are 1,780 gospel quartets in existence, according to Kirksey, and 910 Southern Gospel radio stations are playing the music America loves and believes in.

Southern Gospel reigns.

Wally Fowler (white suit) poses with The Sons of Song, left to right, Bob Robinson, Don Butler, and Calvin Newton, in 1957, just before the ninth anniversary of the first All-Night Gospel Sing.

APPETIZERS

Booth Brothers Vegetable Pizza

2	8-roll packages crescent roll dough
1	egg, beaten
1	8-ounce package cream cheese
1	1-ounce package Hidden Valley dressing mix
1	cup mayonnaise
2/3	cup chopped broccoli
2/3	cup chopped cauliflower
2/3	cup chopped tomatoes
1/2	cup sliced black olives (optional)
3/4	cup shredded cheese
	Other vegetables to taste

The original Booth Brothers started in Detroit with siblings Ron, Charles, Wallace and James. Ron founded the current Booth Brothers with his two sons, Ronnie Booth II and Michael Booth. Ron also sang as a member of The Toney Brothers Quartet and The Rebels Quartet. Based in Tampa, Florida, The Booth Brothers, left to right, are Ronnie, Michael and Ron Booth.

Preheat the oven to 375°. Unroll the crescent rolls and place each triangle about 1 inch apart on a cookie sheet or pizza pan. Spread the beaten egg over each pastry. Bake for about 10 minutes or until golden brown, and let cool.

In a medium bowl mix together the cream cheese, dressing mix, and mayonnaise. Spread the mixture over the rolls. Layer on the remaining ingredients. Return the pizza to the oven to melt the cheeses a little, if desired.

MAKES 16 SLICES.

The Booth Brothers

Crabb Crab Mushrooms

1	6½-ounce can crab meat (or 8 ounces fresh or thawed frozen crab meat, rinsed and drained)
2	teaspoons fresh lemon juice
¼	cup finely chopped black olives
¼	cup mayonnaise
2	tablespoons chopped fresh parsley
¼	teaspoon garlic powder
¼	teaspoon onion powder
	Pinch paprika
24	medium mushrooms, stems removed
	Freshly grated Parmesan cheese

Preheat the oven to 400°. In a medium bowl toss the crab meat with the lemon juice. Add the olives, mayonnaise, parsley, garlic powder, onion powder, and paprika, and mix well. Fill the mushroom caps with the mixture and sprinkle with cheese.

Lightly rinse a baking sheet with water, shaking off the excess water. Place the mushrooms on the sheet. Cover with foil and bake for 12 to 15 minutes. Remove the foil and continue baking about 5 minutes until the tops are golden. Serve immediately.

MAKES 24.

The Crabb Family

The seven-member family group The Crabb Family took home the 1996 Diamond Award Sunrise Group. Their first Top Thirty song, "Ghost Stories," was nominated for song of the year and was written by Gerald Crabb, who also composed their Top Ten single "Where We'll Never Die." Left to right are Terah, Adam, Kelly, Gerald, Kathy, Aaron, and Jason Crabb.

Satisfied Mind Stuffed Mushrooms

1	box large, fresh mushrooms
½	cup (1 stick) butter or margarine, melted
1	6-ounce package Pepperidge Farm stuffing mix
½	cup grated Cheddar cheese
	Salt and pepper to taste

Preheat the oven to 350°. Finely chop the mushrooms. In a medium bowl combine the butter and stuffing mix. Add the cheese and mix well. Add salt and pepper to taste. Stuff the mushrooms with mixture. Place the stuffed mushrooms on a cookie sheet. Bake for 10 to 15 minutes.

SERVES 6 TO 8.
Mike Holcomb • *The Inspirations*

Ed's Favorite Cheese Ball

1	pound Velveeta cheese
⅔	pound Cheddar cheese, grated
2	ounces bleu cheese
2	8-ounce packages cream cheese
1	small onion, grated
1	tablespoon horseradish
1	teaspoon Worcestershire sauce
1½	cups finely chopped pecans or other nuts

In a large bowl combine all of the cheeses and mix together. Cover with foil and let set overnight at room temperature. Add the grated onion, horseradish, and Worcestershire sauce, and mix with a wooden spoon. Refrigerate until firm.

Form into 2 equal-sized balls. Roll each ball in the pecans. Serve at room temperature.

SERVES 12.
Ed Harper • *Harper & Associates*

Uplifting Olive-Filled Cheese Balls

Great for parties and receptions!

½	pound mild Cheddar cheese, softened
2	tablespoons butter
½	cup all-purpose flour
25	stuffed green olives

Preheat the oven to 400°. In a food processor combine the cheese and butter and process until blended. Add the flour and mix until the mixture is the consistency of dough. Knead by hand.

    Wrap about 1 tablespoon of the cheese mixture around each olive. Place the wrapped olives on a baking sheet. Bake for about 12 to 15 minutes. Serve immediately.

MAKES 25.

Janis Lewis Phillips • The Lewis Family

The Lewis Family models their first bus, a 1948 GM "Silverside" that they purchased in 1960. Left to right are Pop, Miggie, Talmadge, Little Roy, Wallace, Polly, and Janis Lewis.

Lily's Chipped Beef Cheese Ball

2   *8-ounce packages cream cheese, softened*

1   *jalapeño pepper, seeded and chopped*

4   *ounces dried chipped beef, finely shredded*

2   *tablespoons mayonnaise*

1   *teaspoon garlic powder*

1½   *cups finely chopped pecans*

In a medium bowl mix together all of the ingredients except for half of the pecans. Form the mixture into a ball. Roll the ball in the remaining pecans.

Variation: To make a dip instead of a ball, add sour cream or more mayonnaise.

MAKES 1 BALL.

Lily Weatherford

The Weatherfords began as a gospel group in 1944 in California. Later they performed for ten years with Rex Humbard in Akron, Ohio. Today Lily Fern Weatherford continues the Weatherford tradition with son Steve, left, and Jamie Caldwell.

The Weatherford Quartet, clockwise from bottom right: Earl Weatherford, Bob Thacker, James Clarke, Lily Fern Weatherford, and Glen Crouse.

Family Circle Cheese Balls

I call this recipe Family Circle after one of our songs because we love to make this at Christmas or Thanksgiving, sit around the table (family circle), play games all night, and eat cheese balls and crackers.

2	8-ounce packages cream cheese, softened
2	cups shredded sharp Cheddar cheese
1	tablespoon chopped pimiento
1	tablespoon chopped onion
1	tablespoon chopped green bell pepper
2	teaspoons Worcestershire sauce
1	teaspoon lemon juice
1	cup finely chopped pecans

In a mixing bowl combine the cream cheese and Cheddar until well blended. Add the pimiento, onion, green pepper, Worcestershire sauce, and lemon juice, and mix well. Chill.
    Shape into 2-inch balls. Roll in the chopped nuts.

MAKES 2 TO 3 DOZEN.

The Kevin Spencer Family

God on the Mountain Sausage Balls

1	pound mild sausage
3	cups Bisquick
3½	to 4 cups (12 to 16 ounces) sharp Cheddar cheese, grated

Preheat the oven to 375°. In a stock pot fry the sausage until browned, and drain well. Remove the pan from the heat. In the same pan, pour the Bisquick over the sausage. Pour the cheese over the Bisquick. Mix well. Turn the mixture onto a floured surface and roll out with a rolling pin. Shape into into 1-inch balls and place on a cookie sheet. Bake for about 8 minutes.

SERVES 15.

Carol Woodard • The McKameys

New River Cheese Sausage Snack

½   cup shortening

2¾   cups self-rising flour

1   pound uncooked hot sausage

4   cups (1 pound) grated sharp Cheddar cheese

Preheat the oven to 375°. In a large bowl cut the shortening into the flour. Add the sausage and cheese and mix well. Shape into small balls and place on a cookie sheet. Bake for 15 to 20 minutes.

MAKES ABOUT 30.

Karen Peck and New River

Karen Peck Gooch performing at the Ryman Auditorium in 1997.

Karen Peck and New River present a unique blend of traditional Southern Gospel and Christian country music. Karen, a soprano who performed with Uncle Alphus LeFevre and sang with The Nelons, formed New River in 1991. Today Karen, her sister Susan Jackson, and lead singer David White offer tight harmonies to the instrumentation of their five-piece band. Left to right are Karen Peck Gooch, Ricky Gooch, Susan Peck Jackson, David White, David Owens, Dale Scragg, Joel Keith, and Craig Nobles.

Radio Days Sausage Cheese Dip

1	*pound hot sausage*
1	*pound lean ground round*
1	*pound light Velveeta cheese*
1	*10-ounce can Ro-tel tomatoes with chopped chilies*
1	*10¾-ounce can cream of mushroom soup*
	Bite-size tortilla chips

In a large skillet cook the meats and drain. Add the Velveeta, tomatoes, and soup, and stir until melted and mixed thoroughly. Serve with bite-size tortilla chips.

SERVES ABOUT 12.

Glen and Van Payne • The Cathedrals

The Cathedrals are one of the most-awarded groups in the history of Southern Gospel music. The popular group is in its fourth decade of spreading the joyful sound. Left to right are Ernie Haase, Scott Fowler, Glen Payne, George Younce, and Roger Bennett.

The Cathedrals

The Cathedrals were founded in 1964 by George Younce and Glen Payne, both gospel singers who began their careers during the heyday of radio. Payne tuned up with The Stamps Quartet on KRLD in Dallas, while Younce was getting primed with The Weatherfords on WOWO in Fort Wayne, Indiana.

Glen and George first got together at the suggestion of televangelist Rex Humbard at a time when The Cathedral Trio sang in the Cathedral of Tomorrow. Younce's coming aboard naturally made the threesome a quartet.

Now thirty-plus years after creation of The Cathedrals, the group is easily one of the most recognizable in all of Southern Gospel. And Younce and Payne have notched more than 100 years of performing between them.

A large measure of their still-growing success is due to the group's legendary bass singer, Younce. The Lenoir, North Carolina, native sang with his first quartet, The Spiritualaires at age fifteen as lead singer. Then his voice changed, and how. Younce has received the *Singing News* Fan Award as favorite Southern Gospel bass eleven times. In 1988 he was named gospel music's Living Legend of the Year, and in 1994 he was inducted into the Gospel Music Museum. He has recorded on more than 100 gospel albums.

Payne, a Texan, attended the Stamps School of Music every summer from 1939 to 1942 and sang with The Stamps Quartet in 1943 and again after World War II ended. He taught in the Stamps School of Music in 1950 and 1951, and the latter year departed The Stamps Quartet to enlist with The Stamps-Ozark Quartet. When that group disbanded in 1956, Payne joined The Weatherford Quartet before moving on to The Rex Humbard Trio, which was to evolve into The Cathedrals.

Payne credits his training as a big reason for his long-term success in music.

"I believe kids nowadays don't know the importance of studying and learning how to sing correctly. I would recommend it highly. If somebody's gonna have a singing career, he has to have a good voice first, and then voice instructors can teach him how to breathe and keep the words out front," Payne says. "Too, I've never had a sore throat from singing. I have never had laryngitis. I attribute that to proper training."

The Cathedrals in the beginning.

The five-part harmony of The Cathedrals of today has earned them many honors, including a total of eleven Dove Awards and eleven Grammy nominations as well as *Singing News* Fans Awards and *Gospel Voice* awards. They were also the first gospel group to appear on NBC's *Today Show* when they sang and chatted with Katie Couric in the fall of 1995.

"It's a compliment that people recognize you for your years and your efforts. But I know who's number one in my life, and that's the Lord. I do it for Him and because of Him. As long as I keep that in mind, then I'm able to accept an award," says Younce. "I never dreamed that our career would be mushrooming like it is at this stage in our lives. I'm overwhelmed with God's touch on my life and His leading in this group."

The Cathedrals spokesman and master of ceremonies has fond memories of the way they recorded albums half a century ago. "Fifty years ago we used to all sing from one microphone. You'd get used to singing in a huddle and with the piano as the only accompaniment. Then we started adding instruments on stage like a bass player to give it a different feel," says Younce.

Times have definitely changed but the popularity of Southern Gospel is one genre of music that is on the rise. "I believe with all my heart that within the next five years, you're going to see the style of music we do more popular than it's ever been," says Younce. "We've got a rhythm and singers better than many country and pop singers. But what we've got, they don't have: lyrics that will make you want to love your neighbor and fall in love with God. Our music is catching on because of the lyrics. As long as we're sincere in what we do, I believe God is going to honor our efforts."

Says Payne, "It's stayed basically the same because of George and I. We basically kept a whole lot of the same sound as a the original Cathedral Quartet. It sounds like The Cathedrals, whether it's thirty years ago or today. I'm proud that we're recognizable and I'm proud we sound a lot like we did in the early days."

Comedian and baritone Mark Lowry of The Gaither Vocal Band.

Popcorn

Buy a bag of Orville Reddenbacher's microwave popcorn. Lay the bag in the microwave this side up (see the bag to locate this side). Preset the microwave for popcorn or read the bag. When it quits heating, wait 2 seconds. Grab the corners—don't grab the middle—and pull. Be careful and don't let the steam burn you. Turn on an *I Love Lucy* rerun and eat the popcorn. It will be the best time you've ever had.

SERVES 1 OR 2.

Mark Lowry

Praise Medley Mexican Cheese Dip

1	cup sour cream
1	cup shredded Cheddar cheese
1	cup shredded Monterey Jack cheese
¼	teaspoon garlic salt
1	4-ounce can chopped green chilies, undrained
	Tortilla chips or raw vegetables

In a blender combine the sour cream, Cheddar, Monterey Jack, garlic salt, and chilies. Cover and blend well. (It will not be creamy or smooth.) Cover and refrigerate for several hours to blend the flavors.

Serve with tortilla chips or raw vegetables.

MAKES 3 CUPS.

Anthony Burger

Anthony Burger is Southern Gospel's most famous pianist. He won the Singing News *Fan Awards Instrumentalist of the Year title ten consecutive years, and thus the award was renamed the Anthony Burger Award. Burger was once a member of The Kingsmen and appears as guest artist and pianist for Bill Gaither concerts.*

Swanee River Freezer Pickles

2   quarts sliced cucumbers

1   medium onion, chopped

2   tablespoons salt

3   cups sugar

1   cup vinegar

In a large bowl mix together the cucumbers and onions. Sprinkle with the salt and let the mixture stand for 2 hours.

   In a saucepan mix the sugar and vinegar and heat to dissolve. Pour the pickles into freezer containers and pour the hot sugar syrup over them. Let cool. Freeze.

MAKES 2 QUARTS.

Willene and Bill Carrier • The Swanee River Boys

The Swanee River Boys brought soft harmony into the fold of gospel music in the late 1930s. The group performed for more than thirty years and sang everything from pop and country to spirituals and gospel. Three of the four members of the group, brothers Buford and Merle Abner and Billy Carrier started out with the Vaughan Four Quartet at WNOX Radio in Knoxville, but a year later the three picked up George Hughes, who had been first tenor with the Texas Rangers Quartet, and formed the Swanee River Boys. The quartet memorized more than 300 tunes and became incredibly popular on radio stations across the Southeast, ranging from Chattanooga, Nashville, and St. Louis to Cincinnati, Charlotte, and Atlanta. Among their most popular tunes were "I've Found a Hiding Place," "Going Up To Be With God," "Jonah," and "Sin Is What's the Matter With the World." The original group disbanded in 1953. Pictured in this early 1940s photograph are, left to right, George Hughes, Buford Abner, Merle Abner, and Bill Carrier.

Gonna Shout All Over Heaven Salsa

4	medium tomatoes
½	cup chopped onion
1	teaspoon chopped garlic
1	tablespoon cilantro
1	teaspoon vinegar
1	teaspoon sugar
	Salt to taste
	Red pepper and Tabasco sauce to taste

In a food processor combine all of the ingredients and process to the desired consistency. Transfer to a serving bowl.

MAKES ABOUT 1 ½ CUPS.

The Cooleys

Haskell Cooley and his wife team as The Cooleys of Wichita, Kansas. They perform a show called A Time for Refreshing *with Haskell on piano and JoLee on bass guitar. Haskell has played piano as a member of The Weatherfords and The Cathedral Quartet earlier in his career. The couple has won numerous awards from the Great Plains Gospel Singing Association and have written such tunes as "I'll Sail Away Home," "Gonna Shout All Over Heaven," and "Singing Easy."*

Spencer's Mountain Seven-Layer Mexican Dip

1	16-ounce can refried beans
1	avocado, mashed with mayonnaise
1	can sliced black olives
1	can chili salsa
½	pound grated Cheddar cheese

Layer the ingredients in a 9 x 13-inch pan or 2 8-inch square pans in the order given. Serve warm or cold with tortilla chips or corn chips.

SERVES ABOUT 8.

Judy Spencer • Manna Music

Chili Con Queso Kirk

6	ounces Velveeta cheese
1	8-ounce package cream cheese
1	8-ounce jar Old El Paso mild picante sauce
	Nacho chips

In a saucepan mix the Velveeta, cream cheese, and picante sauce over low heat. Pour into a serving bowl and serve with chips.

MAKES 3 CUPS.

Kirk Talley

❧ BEVERAGES ❧

Imagine If You Will Orange Julius

1	cup water
1	cup milk
½	cup sugar
1	teaspoon vanilla extract
1	6-ounce can orange juice concentrate
8	to 9 ice cubes

In a blender mix all the ingredients together. Pour into a glass and enjoy. Makes a refreshing summertime drink.

SERVES 1.

Karen Akemon • The Perry Sisters

The Perry Sisters, a group that originated in 1974 in Huntington, West Virginia, are recognized as the only Southern Gospel all-female trio on the charts. Their nickname is "The first ladies of gospel music." Left to right are Tammy Underwood, Diana Gillette, and Karen Akemon.

My Special Tea

1½   cups Tang

½   cup instant lemon tea

1   cup sugar

½   tablespoon ground cinnamon

¼   teaspoon ground cloves

In a medium bowl combine all of the ingredients. Transfer to an airtight container. Use 2 or 3 teaspoons to 1 cup of hot water.

Squire Parsons

Squire Parsons is the former lead singer with The Kingsmen. He also is an accomplished song-writer of gospel music, including the classic "Beulah Land."

Summertime Tea

6 tea bags

4 cups boiling water

1 cup sugar

1 6-ounce can frozen orange juice concentrate, thawed

1 6-ounce can frozen lemonade concentrate, thawed

10 cups cold water

In a pitcher steep the tea bags in the boiling water for 5 minutes. Discard the bags. Add the remaining ingredients and mix well.

MAKES 1 GALLON.

The Booth Brothers

The Booth Brothers harmonize during Spiritfest '96 as brothers Ronnie (left) and Michael gather around father Ron at the microphone.

Singing Praises Punch

This recipe was passed down by my mother.

1   quart water

1   cup sugar

1   tea bag

1   46-ounce can unsweetened pineapple juice

2   cups unsweetened orange juice

     Orange or pineapple sherbet

1   32-ounce bottle ginger ale, chilled

In a 3-quart pan bring the water to a boil with the sugar. Drop in the tea bag and steep according to the strength or color you want. Let cool.

Add the juices. Before serving, transfer the beverage to a punch bowl and add scoops of sherbet. Pour the ginger ale over the sherbet.

MAKES ABOUT 1 GALLON.

Heather Campbell • Executive Director • SGMA Hall of Fame and Museum

Heather Campbell and husband John at the 1997 SGMA Hall of Fame awards banquet in Sevierville, Tennessee.

❧ SOUPS ❧

Granny's October Soup

This recipe makes a ton but freezes well.

1	pound dried Northern beans
4	quarts water
1	pound lean ham, trimmed and cubed
2	ribs celery, chopped
2	carrots, chopped
2	medium potatoes, finely chopped
1	large onion, finely chopped
1	tablespoon chopped pickled jalapeño pepper
1	tablespoon pickled jalapeño pepper juice
1	6-ounce can spicy tomato-vegetable juice
1	4½-ounce can chopped green chilies, undrained
1	tablespoon Worcestershire sauce
½	teaspoon chili powder
½	teaspoon garlic powder

Sort and wash the beans. Place the beans in a Dutch oven, add the water, and let stand for 2 hours.

Bring to a boil, reduce the heat, and simmer for 1 hour. Add the ham, celery, carrots, potatoes, and onion, and simmer for 1 hour. Add the remaining ingredients and simmer for 1 hour or until the beans are tender and the soup has thickened.

Serve with corn bread.

SERVES 10 TO 12, AT LEAST.

Jack and Gail Toney • The Statesmen

Somebody's Coming Soup

When our family moved to Nashville about twenty years ago, all of us plus six other group members lived in the same house. That made ten people. We lived in a four-story duplex apartment with one car among all of us. Sometimes we would go to the grocery store on the bus.

    The kitchen was on the main floor, and Bethany and I would cook meals for all of us. All we could afford was soup. We bought cans and cans of vegetables and tossed them together every week to make soup. Everybody complained and made jokes about the soup, but they ate it anyway. So now, every time we have soup, we all laugh and reminisce about it.

    This is our new recipe for soup.

¾	*of 1 medium onion, sliced*
	Oil or butter
2	*pounds hamburger*
1	*8-ounce can whole kernel corn*
1	*11-ounce can baby lima beans*
1	*8-ounce can black-eyed peas with jalapeños*
1	*14½-ounce can stewed tomatoes*
1	*quart or 1 large package frozen mixed vegetables (I get ones with carrots, broccoli, pasta, water chestnuts, and other vegetables)*
	Salt and pepper to taste

The Telestials' roots go back to 1963 when Beth and her sister formed a trio of women called The Harmony Trio. They made their first record in 1966 in Atlanta, and male vocalists joined the trio in 1969. In the mid-1970s the group earned three Dove nominations. Among their best known songs are "Holy, High, and Lifted Up," "Help Wanted," and "Somebody's Coming." Left to right are Rob Wells, Beth Glass, Caleb Brown, Bethany Brown, and Jerry Brown.

In a skillet sauté the onion in a small amount of oil or butter. Brown the hamburger in the same pan after the onion is finished. Drain. Toss the hamburger and onions in a large soup pot. Add the corn, lima beans, black-eyed peas, and tomatoes, and simmer over medium heat. Cook until the flavors blend together.

    Stir in the frozen mixed vegetables with pasta and finish cooking. Add water along the way as needed for just-right soup.

SERVES 10 TO 12.

The Telestials

Louisiana Duck Gumbo

3	*ducks, cleaned and dressed*
1	*chicken fryer*
1	*pound smoked sausage, chopped*
1	*bunch green onions, diced*
1	*bell pepper, chopped*
3	*ribs celery, chopped*
½	*cup all-purpose flour*
	Salt, black pepper, and cayenne pepper to taste
5	*ounces chopped frozen okra*
⅓	*bottle filé*
1	*package Creole gumbo mix*

In a very large pot boil the ducks and the fryer. Remove the bone and skin, and add the meat back to the stock. (This can even be done the day before and stored in the refrigerator. You can also substitute all fryers for the ducks.)

In an iron skillet brown the sausage. Drain and reserve the drippings. Add the sausage to the stock. Sauté the onion, bell pepper, and celery in some of the sausage drippings. Add to the stock. Pour the remaining sausage drippings in the skillet and brown the flour. Add to the stock. Add salt and peppers to taste. Add the okra and bring to a good boil. Add the filé just before serving and stir very little after that. Serve over hot rice.

You can make it as spicy as you like by adding more cayenne pepper or filé.

SERVES ABOUT 12.

Joel and LaBreeska Hemphill

After their children left the group to pursue their own interest, The Hemphills became a duet once more. Here Joel and LaBreeska share a picnic basket in 1997 in front of Joel's restored 1933 Cadillac.

Tim's Cajun Gumbo

Tim and I are both blessed to be children of parents who were from the State of Louisiana. My mother was full-blooded French who spoke "Cajun French" to her sisters when I was young and they didn't want me to hear what they were talking about. So, of course, along with that heritage, we had gumbo, jambalaya, seafood that my dad had caught with his shrimp boat, and other Southern Cajun dishes.

When I married Tim over thirty years ago, the first gravy I made you could walk across it was so thick! So Tim has really been the "special occasion" cook for our family—like for grilling steaks, barbecuing chickens, or other special dishes that we serve when we have guests. I would be responsible for all the other dishes, setting the table, and seeing that everything in the house looked in order.

On Tim's 50th birthday, Angelina and I decided that instead of black balloons and an "over the hill" party, we would invite about twenty or thirty of our closest friends and we would have a special supper. So we designated Tim to fix the Cajun Gumbo we all have loved for years.

We purchased six chickens and all the ingredients. Tim made the roux for the gravy and finished the gumbo the day before, so it could set in the refrigerator all night to let the ingredients come together for the best taste. He added cayenne pepper as usual. Then he saw lemon pepper in the cabinet. Since we had used it on chicken in another recipe, he made the decision to use it on this occasion, too. Then he must have looked up and seen the Tabasco sauce, and, since he was making gallons of gumbo, he added that also.

Tim then put the gumbo in the refrigerator and the next day took it out to let it simmer on the stove while the rice was cooking. When the lid was taken off, the entire house had a hot and sour smell!! We immediately panicked. Guests were on their way. We did not have time to do anything. Angelina stood at the door greeting people with a can of Lysol in her hand and spraying away as she explained to each guest.

I watched with amusement at our guests that night. They tried to be gracious. They would taste a spoonful...and I would see it hit them. They would try to straighten their faces. I wonder why so much potato salad, crackers, corn bread, and desserts were consumed that night!

Tim took the boned chicken out of the gravy, put it in a colander, and rinsed it with water, but could not get the sour taste and smell out of it. We just had to throw it away.

We never let him forget this. In fact, he has received several gifts of lemon pepper for Christmas since then. I believe he will never again experiment when guests are coming and will always "follow the receipt!"—Dixie McKeithen

1   cup wheat flour

1   chicken, boiled, skinned, and boned

     Shrimp and sausage (optional)

1   cup chopped bell pepper

1   onion, chopped

½   cup chopped celery

2   tablespoons gumbo filé powder

2   tomatoes, diced (optional)

2   tablespoons salt

1   tablespoon red cayenne pepper

2   quarts water

Brown the flour (stirring often) on a baking sheet in an oven, or brown it in a skillet with ¼ cup of oil, stirring constantly until it turns a chocolate brown. (Brown flour mix can sometimes be picked up at the grocery store.)

In a stock pot combine all of the ingredients and cook for 45 minutes. Serve over cooked rice like soup.

SERVES 6.

Tim McKeithen • The McKeithens

The McKeithens began their career when husband and wife Tim and Dixie performed as part of The Hemphill Family. But once daughter Angelina was ready to join her mom and dad on the stage, The McKeithens became a family act. Besides her vocal abilities, Angelina plays numerous instruments, including guitar, bass, drums, keyboards, mandolin, banjo, and harmonica. Left to right are Tim, Angelina, and Dixie McKeithen.

Masters Mushroom-Broccoli Soup

1   14½-ounce can chicken broth

5   ounces frozen chopped broccoli

2   tablespoons margarine

1½   cups sliced fresh mushrooms

½   cup chopped onion

2   tablespoons all-purpose flour

½   teaspoon salt

⅛   teaspoon pepper

1¼   cups milk

1   8-ounce can whole kernel corn, drained

1   tablespoon chopped pimiento

In a saucepan bring the broth and broccoli to a boil. Reduce the heat, cover, and simmer for 5 minutes. Set aside.

    In a separate saucepan or skillet melt the margarine and sauté the mushrooms and onions. Blend in the flour, salt, and pepper. Add the milk and cook, stirring constantly, until thickened. Cook and stir 2 more minutes. Add the broccoli with broth, corn, and pimiento. Heat for 3 minutes.

SERVES 6.

Hovie Lister • The Statesmen

Hovie Lister is the sensational showman and piano man behind The Statesmen.

Hovie Lister and the Statesmen Quartet

Begun on October 19, 1948, the sensational Statesmen were organized by the incomparable showman Hovie Lister. Wrote Furman Bishop, sports editor of *The Atlanta Journal* in an article for the *Saturday Evening Post,* "He (Hovie Lister) put the rhythm into religion."

Lister, of Greenville, South Carolina, learned the basics of Southern Gospel music from his grandfather, who taught the old-time ten-day singing school, and his first job in music was with his four uncles who performed as The Lister Brothers Quartert.

In 1943 Lister attended the Stamps-Baxter School of Music in Dallas to study piano, and then moved to Atlanta where for several years he played for The Homeland Harmony, The LeFevre Trio, and The Rangers Quartet.

Lister's original Statesmen included himself as manager, pianist, and emcee; lead singer Mosie Lister (no relation); first tenor Bobby Strickland, baritone Bervin Kendrick; and bass singer Gordon Hill.

When Mosie and Hill left a year later, Hovie obtained the services of Jake Hess as lead singer and Aycel Soward to sing bass, but Soward didn't hang around for long, so Hovie got Jim S. ("Big Chief") Wetherington to take his place.

Then after Strickland left the group, Cat Freeman stepped in as first tenor. The Statesmen whipped their act into shape as they practiced every song to perfection and even rehearsed choreography and stage entrances together. Later, Hovie was drafted into the Army and the group got Doy Ott to take over as pianist. When Hovie returned, Ott gave up the keyboard and filled in at baritone as Kendrick left the act. Finally, Freeman decided to move on and Hovie put Denver Crumpler in his place. Now The Statesmen were ready to explode on the Southern Gospel scene.

From the very beginning the style of The Statesmen was "rare back and sing." And that they did. But there were other accolades that made them one of the biggest groups in Southern Gospel.

Hovie's Statesmen were the first Southern Gospel group to have a nationwide radio show as well as a syndicated television show, *Singin' Time in Dixie.* Their vocal talents were also called upon to perform the title song for the soundtrack of the feature film *A Man Called Peter.*

Today, some fifty years after their birth, The Statesmen continue their tradition with Lister, Jack Toney, Wallace Nelms, Mike LoPrinzi, and Doug Young.

Toney, a native of Boaz, Alabama, besides having such a great voice, has penned more than four hundred songs and has been the inspiration for many young men who have entered the field of gospel music.

Tenor Nelms hails from Kingsport, Tennessee, and is college trained in music and computer science and is a retiree from Eastman Kodak Company. He is an active member of the Gideons International and is a songwriter.

Baritone singer LoPrinzi is from Ravenswood, West Virginia, and studied music and Bible at United Wesleyan College. The singer-songwriter has also been a member of The Plainsmen Quartet and The Blackwood Brothers, among other groups.

Bass singer Young of Huntsville, Alabama, has been performing in gospel music since 1968. He played bass guitar for Aaron Wilburn and played guitar and sang bass with The Regents Quartet for several years. Also a businessman, Young leases cranes out of Huntsville and custom coach buses out of Nashville.

Cheerful Noise Cheese Corn Chowder

2½	cups water
1½	cups peeled and chopped potatoes
1	cup sliced carrots
1	cup chopped celery
½	cup chopped onion
1½	teaspoons salt
¼	teaspoon pepper
¼	cup butter
¼	cup all-purpose flour
2	cups milk
2½	cups shredded Cheddar cheese
1	16-ounce can creamed corn

In a large saucepan combine the water, potatoes, carrots, celery, onion, salt, and pepper. Bring to a boil. Simmer for 15 minutes or until the vegetables are tender.

In a separate saucepan melt the butter, stir in the flour, and cook until bubbly. Gradually add the milk, stirring constantly. Bring to a boil and cook 1 minute more. Add the cheese and stir until melted. Gradually add the cheese sauce to the soup. Stir in the corn and heat through. Serve and enjoy!

SERVES ABOUT 6.

Jo (Mrs. Herman) Harper • Harper & Associates

Les Beasley, left, and Herman Harper enjoy a few leisure moments at the National Quartet Convention in the fall of 1971.

Jim's Alabama Chili

I've always enjoyed chili. Since leaving Alabama years ago, I have tasted just about every version you can think of—and they have all been very good. But my favorite chili is still the one that my mother and sisters made back in Alabama. I remember all of us sitting down to a dinner of chili and Southern-style corn bread. So not only do I find this chili my favorite, but eating it brings back fond memories of my family and Alabama. I hope you enjoy it, too.

1	*pound ground beef*
2	*tablespoons fat*
1	*teaspoon salt*
2	*to 3 tablespoons chili powder*
1	*8-ounce can tomato sauce*
1	*20-ounce can red kidney beans*
1	*medium onion, finely chopped*
2	*tablespoons vinegar*
½	*teaspoon garlic powder*
1	*28-ounce can tomatoes*

In a stock pot heat the fat, then quickly brown the meat, stirring with a fork. Add the remaining ingredients and mix well. Cover and simmer, stirring occasionally, for 30 to 45 minutes.

SERVES 4.

Jim Nabors

This Mayberry trio could go on the road as Taylor, Pyle, and Fife, if only that didn't sound so much like Peter, Pyle, and Mary. Jim Nabors (left) sings with 1997 Grammy-award-winning Southern Gospel singer Andy Griffith (center) and Don Knotts as part of a '60s television special.

None Better Chili Beans

The best chili this side of Pecos!

3	pounds ground chuck
½	green bell pepper, chopped
1	large onion, chopped
2	1¾-ounce envelopes Chili-o with onion
1	28-ounce can whole tomatoes
3	16-ounce cans light red kidney beans
	Dash of chili powder
	Salt and pepper to taste

In a large saucepan brown the ground chuck, green pepper, and onion until the chuck is done. Add the remaining ingredients and let simmer to your individual taste—the longer, the better.

SERVES 10.

Mary Cleary

"SPEER-IT" AWARDS
Match the Speer with the year he or she was inducted into the Gospel Music Association Hall of Fame:

1. G.T. "Dad" Speer	A. 1972
2. Lena Brock "Mom" Speer	B. 1975
3. Brock Speer	C. 1995
4. Ben Speer	D. 1971

Answers
1. D, 2. A, 3. B, 4. C

❧ SALADS ❧

Heavenly Seven-Layer Salad

1	head lettuce, chopped
1	head cauliflower, chopped
1	red onion, diced
1	10-ounce package frozen green peas, thawed to room temperature
2	cups light mayonnaise
8	ounces Parmesan cheese
1	3-ounce jar bacon bits

In a large glass bowl layer the ingredients in the order given. Cover the bowl with plastic wrap and refrigerate until ready to serve.

Stir together and serve.

SERVES 6 TO 8.

Jackie Leach • Harper & Associates

Jackie and Tony Leach and their daughter, Peyton.

Special Seven-Layer Salad

½   head lettuce

1   cup chopped green bell pepper

1   cup chopped celery

½   cup chopped green onion

1   10-ounce package frozen peas

1   cup mayonnaise

1   jar real bacon bits

1½   cups grated Cheddar cheese

In an oblong glass pan layer the ingredients in the order listed. Cover with plastic wrap and refrigerate until ready to serve.

SERVES 6.

The McGruders

The McGruders features the husband and wife team of Carroll and Priscilla McGruder. The group was nominated for a Gospel Music Association award in 1990 for their song "I Just Started Living." Based in Kennett, Missouri, where Carroll is a pastor who preaches every Sunday, The McGruders have won awards from Cash Box Magazine and The Singing News. Among their top songs are "Special," "Saved by Grace," and "Bloodbought." Left to right are Carroll McGruder, Priscilla McGruder, and Denny Autry.

Testifying Taco Salad

1   pound ground beef, cooked and well drained

1   16-ounce can red kidney beans, drained

1   large avocado (optional)

1   head lettuce, chopped

8   ounces Longhorn cheese, grated

1   bottle Thousand Island dressing

1   medium onion, chopped

2   small tomatoes

1   16-ounce bag nacho chips, crushed

In a large serving bowl mix all of the ingredients together. Serve.

SERVES 6.

Linda Rawlings

Jerry's Special Salad

This salad always gets raves when we serve it.

1   small head lettuce, chopped

2   ribs celery, diced small

1   small bunch green onions, chopped small (tops and all)

1   medium to large ripe tomato, diced (use juice of tomato, too)

    Salt to taste

    Coarse black pepper (we use lots)

In a serving bowl combine all of the ingredients and mix well.

    The secret to this salad is the freshness of the ingredients and the mixing. You must mix and mix and mix and mix. This will create a juice in the salad and it will not require any salad dressing at all.

SERVES 4.

Jerry Goff

Answer the Call Cauliflower Salad

1	large head cauliflower
9	to 10 crisp bacon strips, crumbled
¾	cup Parmesan cheese
1	large onion, sliced and chopped
½	cup sugar
1	head lettuce, broken
1	to 1½ cups mayonnaise

In a large bowl layer the ingredients in the order given. Cover with plastic wrap and refrigerate overnight. Toss before serving.

SERVES 6 TO 8.

Bonnie R. (Mrs. "Little Roy") Lewis • The Lewis Family

Photo by Lance LeRoy

The Lewis Family gathers around the canopied wagon, built in 1850, which Pop rode to church in his early childhood, 1905 to 1910. Restored in 1984, it still has its original canvas umbrella top. From left to right are Wallace Lewis, Pop, Little Roy, Mom, Lewis Phillips, Travis Lewis (standing in wagon), Janis Lewis-Phillips, Polly Lewis-Copsey, and Miggie Lewis.

Grocery Store Salad

This will keep for several days in the refrigerator.

Salad:

> *1 head cabbage*
>
> *Bell pepper*
>
> *Radishes*
>
> *Celery*
>
> *Onion*
>
> *Tomatoes*
>
> *Cucumber*

Sauce:

½ cup chili sauce

½ cup tarragon vinegar

½ cup vegetable oil

> *Sugar to taste*
>
> *Salt and pepper to taste*

The Speer Family in the 1960s revolves around Dad Speer (center). Clockwise from top center are Ann Downing, Mom Speer, Charles Yates, Ben Speer, Brock Speer, and Faye Speer.

Chop all vegetables. In a serving bowl mix the vegetables together.

In a small bowl or container mix together the chili sauce, vinegar, oil, sugar, salt, and pepper, and pour over the vegetables.

SERVES 6.

Rosa Nell Speer Powell

Tennessee Summer Salad

Salad:

1　head romaine lettuce, washed and chopped

1　bunch green onions, finely chopped

2　11-ounce cans mandarin oranges, drained

1　pint fresh strawberries, sliced

4　ounces sliced almonds, glazed (see below)

Dressing:

½　cup rice vinegar

¼　cup olive oil

　　Sugar to taste

In a large bowl mix the lettuce, onions, oranges, strawberries, and almonds.

In a blender combine the vinegar, olive oil, and sugar to taste, and blend until smooth. Pour over the salad before serving.

Note: To glaze the almonds, place them in a heavy frying pan, cover lightly with sugar, and stir over low heat until brown.

SERVES 4 TO 6.

Cleon Dewey • The Deweys

The Deweys, left to right, Suzanne, Levoy, Cleon, and Cindy, began performing in the summer of 1967. (They have performed in more than thirty countries.) Today the family works together in a TV show, Let's Sing America, *while Levoy and Cleon continue to write songs, produce albums, and travel.*

George's Tabasco Cole Slaw

⅓   cup vinegar

¼   cup salad oil

2   tablespoons sugar

2   tablespoons onion flakes

1   teaspoon salt

1   teaspoon dry mustard

½   teaspoon celery salt

¼   teaspoon Tabasco sauce

4   cups grated cabbage (red and/or green)

1   carrot, grated

¼   cup chopped green bell pepper

In a large bowl combine the vinegar, oil, sugar, onion flakes, salt, dry mustard, celery salt, and Tabasco sauce. Mix well. Add the cabbage, carrot, and green pepper. Toss again before serving.

SERVES 4.

George Younce • The Cathedrals

The Cathedrals' George Younce models his red hot chili pepper while he whips up a dish in the kitchen.

George Younce on stage.

Lulu's Chicken Salad

This is so yummy that it will get lots of compliments.

3   *or 4 chicken breasts, cooked and cubed (you can use canned chicken if you're in a hurry)*

       Salt and pepper to taste

½   *teaspoon paprika*

1   *tablespoon seasoning salt*

2   *ribs celery, diced into medium-sized pieces*

1   *small bag slivered almonds, toasted*

1   *cup whipping cream, whipped stiff*

1   *cup Miracle Whip*

1   *11-ounce can mandarin oranges, drained*

In a medium bowl mix the chicken, salt, pepper, paprika, and seasoning salt. Add the celery and almonds. In a separate bowl mix together the whipped cream and Miracle Whip. Add the dressing mixture to the chicken mixture. Add the mandarin oranges last and toss lightly. Chill for 2 to 3 hours.

    Variation: You can substitute green seedless grapes for the oranges, if preferred.

SERVES 4 TO 6.

Lulu Roman

Lulu Roman combines the humor from her years on Hee Haw *with her sparkling vocal talents as a singer and recording artist for Daywind Records. She won the Gospel Music Association Dove Award for album by a secular artist in 1984 for* You Were Loving Me.

Bobby's Homemade Chicken Salad

4	large skinless chicken breasts
¼	onion, chopped
4	dill pickles, finely chopped
4	sweet pickles, finely chopped
2	hard-boiled eggs
1	rib celery, chopped
1	teaspoon pimiento
¼	teaspoon salt
¼	teaspoon pepper
	Mayonnaise
	Miracle Whip salad dressing

Boil the chicken breasts until done and then chop into fine pieces.

In a medium bowl combine the chicken, onion, pickles, eggs, celery, pimiento, salt, and pepper. Add the mayonnaise and salad dressing in equal parts to the desired thickness and consistency.

SERVES 4.

Bobby Goodman • The Happy Goodman Family

This 1970s version of The Happy Goodman Family featured, clockwise from top left, Sam Goodman, Ernie Maxwell, Ricky Goodman, Howard Goodman, Bob Goodman, Vestal Goodman, and Rusty Goodman.

There Is a Peace Pasta Salad

¼ cup fresh lemon juice (approximately 2 large lemons)

¼ cup canola oil

4 teaspoons sugar

1½ teaspoons salt (or to taste)

2 teaspoons hot pepper sauce

1 pound package spiral pasta (such as fusilli), cooked according to package directions and drained

¼ cup sliced green onions

1 cup grated carrots

1 bunch fresh broccoli florets

½ cup chopped green bell pepper

½ cup chopped red bell pepper

2 teaspoons Italian dressing

In a large bowl combine the lemon juice, oil, green onions, sugar, salt, and hot pepper sauce. Mix well. Add the hot pasta and toss. Add the remaining ingredients, and mix well. Chill.

SERVES 4 TO 6.

John Starnes

John Starnes began his gospel career singing during Jimmy Swaggart crusades across the world. During his thirteen years with Swaggart's organization, Starnes was the evangelist's personal pilot. Today he performs as a successful solo act.

Raspberry Delight

1	*10-ounce package marshmallows*
1	*10-ounce package raspberries*
1	*8 ounce package cream cheese, softened*
²⁄₃	*cup mayonnaise*
½	*pint whipped cream*

In a double boiler melt the marshmallows with the raspberries. In a small bowl mix the cream cheese and mayonnaise. Add to the raspberry mixture. Cool.

Add the whipped cream and mix well. Place in a 1-inch deep dish and freeze until firm.

SERVES 6 TO 8.

Margo and Holly Smith

The most prominent mother-daughter duet in gospel is Margo Smith and Holly, left. Margo is also a country music star and well-known among her fans for her yodeling abilities.

Mansion Over the Hilltop Molded Cheese Salad

1	16-ounce can crushed pineapple
¾	cups sugar
2	envelopes unflavored gelatin
1	cup cold water
	Juice of 1 lemon
½	cup chopped nuts
1½	cups grated Longhorn cheese
½	pint whipping cream

In a saucepan heat the pineapple and sugar. Add the gelatin, water, and lemon juice while hot. Stir to dissolve the gelatin, and then let cool.

In a medium bowl fold the nuts and cheese into the whipped cream. Fold the whipped cream mixture into the pineapple mixture. Pour into a 2-inch deep dish and refrigerate overnight to cool and set.

SERVES 6.

Van and Glen Payne • The Cathedrals

Sunshine Salad

This recipe was passed down by my grandmother.

2	cups water
2	3-ounce boxes lemon gelatin
1	cup pineapple juice
1	8-ounce can crushed pineapple
1	cup grated carrots

In a saucepan bring the water to a boil. Add the gelatin and stir to dissolve. Add the pineapple juice. Pour into a dish or gelatin mold and let gel slightly. Add the crushed pineapple and the carrots. Refrigerate until set completely.

Serve on a lettuce leaf.

SERVES 6 TO 8.

Heather Campbell • Executive Director • SGMA Hall of Fame and Museum

Ring Those Bells Frozen Salad

1	16-ounce carton sour cream
2	tablespoons lemon juice
¾	cup sugar
⅛	teaspoon salt
1	9-ounce can crushed pineapple
¼	cup maraschino cherries
1	banana, cut in quarters

Line a muffin tin with paper liners. In a large bowl combine all of the ingredients and mix well. Pour into the prepared paper liners. Freeze for several hours.

Remove the paper and serve on a lettuce leaf. Let the salads set for 10 to minutes before serving.

MAKES 12.

Judy Spencer • Manna Music

Judy Spencer of Manna Music, one of Southern Gospel's top song publishing companies (including the classic "How Great Thou Art," "God on the Mountain," and "Come on Ring Those Bells"), shares a moment with Christian and Western greats Roy Rogers and Dale Evans during the couple's fiftieth wedding anniversary celebration in Victorville, California, in 1997.

Mighty Fine Pineapple Salad

This was Roger and Kirk's grandmother's recipe.

2	*whole eggs*
½	*cup sugar*
2	*tablespoons all-purpose flour*
4	*slices canned pineapple, cubed; reserve juice*
4	*ounces American cheese, grated*
1	*cup miniature marshmallows*
	Grated cheese for topping

In the top of a double boiler beat together the eggs, sugar, flour, and 1 cup of pineapple juice. (If there is not enough juice for 1 cup, make up the difference with water.) Cook the mixture over simmering water, stirring constantly, until thick. Let cool for a few minutes.

Add the pineapple cubes, cheese, and marshmallows. Chill, top with grated cheese, and serve.

SERVES 4.

The Talley Trio

The Talleys were one of the most popular groups of the 1980s with members Kirk, Roger, and Debra Talley. The trio disbanded in 1993 but when Roger and Debra's daughter Lauren began developing her vocal talents it was only natural for a new Talley trio to emerge. Appropriately they called themselves The Talley Trio. Left to right are Roger, Debra, and Lauren.

Mom Jones' Yeast Rolls

1	¼-ounce envelope dry yeast
½	cup water
½	cup sugar
1½	cups warm water
3	tablespoons oil
2	teaspoons salt
2	eggs
2	cups all-purpose flour

In a small bowl mix the yeast and ½ cup of warm water, and let set while mixing the rest of the ingredients.

In a large bowl mix the sugar, 1½ cups of warm water, oil, and salt. Beat and add the eggs. Add the yeast mixture. Begin adding the flour, and continue until you can work with the dough. Place the dough in the greased bowl, cover, and let rise until doubled.

Punch down the dough and place in the refrigerator.

When ready to use, shape the dough into rolls and place in a pan. Let the rolls rise. (I usually let them rise for about 2 hours.) Bake at 400° until golden brown.

MAKES ABOUT 2 DOZEN ROLLS.

Susan Jobe • National Quartet Convention

Beasley Family Biscuits

3   cups Martha White self-rising flour with Hot Rize

2   teaspoons baking powder

3   tablespoons cooking oil

1½   cups buttermilk

Preheat the oven to 450°. In a medium bowl mix the flour and baking powder. Add the oil and mix. Add the buttermilk, and stir until the mixture is nice and smooth. Sprinkle waxed paper with flour and then turn the dough onto the waxed paper. Flip the dough over one time. Pat lightly, and spread out to about 1-inch thick. Cut with a glass or biscuit cutter.

    Cover the bottom of an 8 x 11-inch baking dish with cooking oil. Flip each biscuit over one time in the oil so that both sides will be coated. Arrange the biscuits in the pan so they touching each other. (That makes them rise better.) Use a dish that will be filled with biscuits. Do not have any vacant space between the biscuits. Bake in the preheated oven on the top rack for about 30 minutes or until browned.

MAKES ABOUT 2 DOZEN BISCUITS.

Mr. and Mrs. Les Beasley

Gathering for the TV sponsor are Florida Boys, left to right, Coy Cook, Glen Allred, Steve Sanders, Darrell Stewart, J.G. Whitfield, and Les Beasley.

This vintage photo of The Florida Boys shows Hal Kennedy (at the microphone) backed by Darrell Stewart, Steve Sanders, Gene McDonald, Glen Allred, and Les Beasley.

The Florida Boys

The year 1997 marked the fiftieth anniversary of the origins of The Florida Boys, one of gospel's top acts and the only male quartet that has been consistently popular for the past half century.

The group, based in Pensacola, Florida, has recorded more than 100 albums behind the strength of the voices of lead singer Les Beasley, baritone Glen Allred, pianist Darrell Stewart, and bass singer Buddy Liles. Tenor Allan Cox joined the group in late 1997.

The Florida Boys have won numerous Dove Awards and *Singing News* Fan Awards but are also famous as the first gospel group to have a nationally syndicated television program, *The Gospel Singing Jubilee*, with more than 500 episodes that began airing in 1964 and ran for eighteen years.

Allred became the first of the "modern" Florida Boys in 1952 when he joined what was known as The Gospel Melody Quartet, established in 1947 by J.G. Whitfield. Glen, just a teenager at the time, had already performed with such acts as Wally Fowler and The Oak Ridge Quartet. One year later, in 1953, Beasley, an ex-Marine tank platoon commander, came aboard.

Then came pianist Stewart (1956), famed for his red socks, bass singer Liles (1972), and tenor Greg Cook, and multi-instrumentalist Tim Lovelace.

Fowler, famous as a Southern gospel promoter among his other hats, referred to the group as "the boys from Florida with sand in their shoes and a song in their heart."

The songs in their hearts as well as on the charts have included the Number One hits "Standing on the Solid Rock," "When He Was on the Cross," "Lead Me to the Altar," and "I Lean on You, Lord."

The Florida Boys enter their second half century of making gospel music in 1998. Humor marks a part of the act for "the boys from Florida with sand in their shoes and a song in their heart." Surrounding Les Beasley are, clockwise from top left, Allan Cox, Buddy Liles, Glen Allred, and Darrell Stewart.

"We want our audiences to have a good time. That's important. But we also want them to hear what we're saying in the songs," says Beasley, who was instrumental in founding the Gospel Music Association and is president of the National Quartet Convention. "It's all about teamwork. Singers may come and go, but God never changes. His voice is as clear today as it was fifty years ago."

Beasley conceived the idea of the Dove Award and designed it with artist Bob McConnell.

The King Is Coming Wheat Bread

½   cup warm water

1   teaspoon sugar

1   ¼-ounce package dry yeast

⅛   teaspoon ginger

2   teaspoons vegetable oil

2   teaspoons honey

1   15-ounce can condensed milk

1   cup whole wheat flour

3   cups unbleached white flour

In the bowl of an electric mixer combine the water, sugar, yeast, and ginger. Add the oil, honey, and sweetened condensed milk, and mix together. In a separate bowl combine the whole wheat flour and all-purpose flour. Add the flours to the liquid mixture, adding the final cup by hand.

Divide the dough among 2 well-greased 1-pound coffee cans or 1 2-pound can. Grease the plastic lids and seal the cans. Let the dough rise until the lids pop off.

Preheat the oven to 330° to 350°. Bake the bread in the cans for 30 to 40 minutes or until golden brown.

Let cool slightly before removing the bread from the cans.

MAKES 2 LOAVES.

Bill and Gloria Gaither

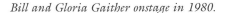

Bill and Gloria Gaither onstage in 1980.

Gloria Gaither is an author, lyricist, teacher, and speaker, who has written twelve books and more than six hundred songs, including "Because He Lives," "The King Is Coming," and "Something About That Name." A member of The Gaither Trio, she has written the lyrics to twenty Dove Award-winning songs.

Eva's Corn Bread

¾   cup self-rising cornmeal

⅔   cup buttermilk

1   egg

2   tablespoons oil

Preheat the oven to 475°. Cover the bottom of an 8-inch square pan with oil and heat in the oven for 8 to 10 minutes.

   In a medium bowl combine the remaining ingredients. Pour some of the hot oil into the mixture and stir. Pour the batter into the remaining hot oil in the pan and bake for 20 minutes.

SERVES 6.

Eva Mae LeFevre

When piano-playing Eva Mae Whittington married Urias LeFevre in the early 1930s, the combination of Eva Mae and brothers Urias and Alphus LeFevre made The LeFevres one of the most popular gospel groups of their time. Their 1940 recording of "Beautiful Flowers" sold fifty thousand copies in ten days.

The LeFevres first made their mark on Southern Gospel in the 1920s as the sibling LeFevre Trio with brothers Urias and Alphus and sister Maude LeFevre. Later Maude left but Eva Mae Whittington married into the group, and the trio kept plugging. After moving to Atlanta in 1939, The LeFevres became incredibly popular and owned their own building and twenty-four track recording studio and had their own TV show. Here the family group poses beside their bus in the 1960s, just a few years before they sold their act to Rex Nelon.

Dottie's Corn Bread

This is such a moist bread. It is excellent served with fresh turnips, turnip greens, any kind of dried beans, poke salad, cabbage, and stew. It can also be used for dressing.

1   tablespoon shortening
      Small amount of cornmeal
½   cup shortening
2½   cups self-rising cornmeal
¾   cup self-rising flour
1   tablespoon sugar
1   egg
½   teaspoon salt
½   teaspoon baking powder
      Buttermilk

Perhaps the most prolific female songwriter of Southern Gospel is Kentuckian Dottie Rambo with more than seven hundred songs to her credit.

Preheat the oven to 375°. Spray an iron skillet with nonstick cooking spray. Melt 1 tablespoon of shortening in the skillet in the oven. Sprinkle with a thin layer of cornmeal and let brown. Set aside.

In a saucepan melt ½ cup of shortening. Add the cornmeal, flour, sugar, egg, salt, and baking powder. Add enough buttermilk to make the consistency of pancake batter. Pour the batter into the skillet immediately (before it rises). Bake for 20 minutes on the top rack of the oven. After 20 minutes, shake the skillet to see if it is done in the middle.

When the corn bread is done, turn the oven dial to broil and quickly brown. Remove from the oven and let cool for 5 to 10 minutes.

Shake the skillet to loosen the corn bread before cutting.

Variation: For added variety, just add ½ cup of whole kernel corn and ½ cup of cracklin's to make cracklin' corn bread, which is a famous recipe of the Kentucky Hills people.

SERVES 6 TO 8.

Dottie Rambo

Dottie Rambo is one of Southern Gospel's top tunesmiths and has been writing songs since the age of eight or nine. The daughter of a blind Pentecostal preacher, she taught herself to play guitar and by age sixteen was an accomplished lead guitarist.

Jack's Never-Fail Corn Bread

1   cup self-rising cornmeal

     Dash salt

1   tablespoon cooking oil

     Milk or buttermilk (enough to make a thin batter)

2   tablespoons cooking oil

Preheat the oven to 425°. In a mixing bowl combine the cornmeal, salt, 1 tablespoon of oil, and milk and stir until well blended. Set aside. In a seasoned iron skillet on the range top, heat the 2 tablespoons of cooking oil until very hot. Pour the batter into the hot skillet while it's still on the burner. Wait a few seconds until the batter sizzles, and then place the skillet in the hot oven. Bake about 25 minutes until golden brown. Turn the bread over and return to the pan. Slice it like a pie.

SERVES 8.

Jack Toney • The Statesmen

Jack and Gail Toney pose with the love of their lives, their Maltese JeeGee. Jack, who sings with The Statesmen, is an avid home gardener and loves growing lettuce, onions, peppers, and his prized tomatoes.

Cornucopia Corn Bread

3	cups cornmeal
1	cup all-purpose flour
4	jalapeño peppers, crushed
3	tablespoons salt
2	eggs
3	teaspoons salt
2	eggs
3	teaspoons baking powder
½	cup oil
1	large onion, chopped
1	15-ounce can creamed corn
1⅔	cups milk
1½	cups Longhorn cheese, grated

Preheat the oven to 400°. Grease a 9 x 13-inch pan. In a large bowl combine all of the ingredients, and mix well. Pour the batter into the prepared pan. Bake for 45 minutes.

SERVES 8 TO 12.

Susan Jobe • National Quartet Convention

Beckie's Mexican Corn Bread

2	tablespoons butter
2	cups yellow self-rising cornmeal
2	tablespoons sugar
2	eggs
1½	cups milk
1	15-ounce can cream-style corn
1	cup shredded cheese
¼	cup butter
	Jalapeño peppers (optional)

Preheat the oven to 450°. In an 8-inch square pan melt 2 tablespoons of butter. In a large bowl combine the cornmeal, sugar, eggs, and milk. Add the corn, cheese, ¼ cup of butter, and the peppers, and blend well. Pour into the pan and bake for 30 minutes or until brown on top.

SERVES ABOUT 6.

Beckie Simmons • BSA Talent Agency

HIGH-FLYING DOVES
Match the artist with their Dove Award-winning album:

1.	The Speers	A.	*Then and Now*
2.	The Kingsmen	B.	*Between the Cross and Heaven*
3.	The Cathedrals	C.	*Workin'*
4.	The Rex Nelon Singers	D.	*From Out of the Past*
5.	The Hemphills	E.	*We Shall Behold the King*
6.	The Martins	F.	*Southern Classics*
7.	The Gaither Vocal Band	G.	*Wherever You Are*

Answers
1.B, 2.D, 3.A, 4.E, 5.C, 6.G, 7.F

Fox Family Turkey Corn Bread Dressing

This recipe has been in our family for over seventy-five years.

1	skillet corn bread, baked and crumbled
4	hamburger buns or 10 slices white bread, crumbled
1	rib celery, chopped
1	4-ounce can sliced mushrooms
1	$10\frac{3}{4}$-ounce can cream of mushroom soup
1	onion, chopped
1	8-ounce can sliced water chestnuts
2	tablespoons sage
3	cups turkey broth
	Salt and pepper to taste
2	hard-boiled eggs, chopped

Preheat the oven to 350°. In a large bowl stir together all of the ingredients except the hard-boiled eggs, and mix well. Spread half of the mixture in a 9 x 13-inch pan. Spread the chopped eggs over the mixture, and then top with the remaining mixture. Bake for 50 minutes.

SERVES 6.

Mildred Fox, mother • The Fox Brothers

I Go to the Rock of Ages Mushroom Bread

1   8-ounce package refrigerated crescent roll dough

1   pint fresh mushrooms, sliced

3   tablespoons butter or margarine, melted

¼   cup grated Parmesan cheese

¼   teaspoon Italian seasoning

Preheat the oven to 375°. Separate the dough into triangles and place them on a 13-inch baking stone with points in the center. Press the crescent roll dough together and pinch the seams together.

    In a small skillet melt the butter and sauté the mushrooms. Spread the mushrooms on top of the dough. Sprinkle with the Parmesan cheese and herbs. Bake for 15 to 20 minutes. Cut into wedges or squares with a pizza cutter and serve warm.

MAKES 12 SERVINGS OR 24 SMALLER SERVINGS.

The Kingdom Heirs

The Kingdom Heirs have entertained full time at Dollywood theme park in Pigeon Forge, Tennessee, since 1986. Today they sing to more people each year than any other gospel group. Clockwise from bottom left are Jamie Graves, Dennis Murphy, Steve French, Eric Bennett, Arthur Rice, Kreis French, and David Sutton.

Inspirational Blueberry Muffins

This recipe comes from my mother, Faye Hutchins. We grow our own blueberries.

¾	cup all-purpose flour
¾	cup whole wheat flour
½	cup firmly packed brown sugar
1	teaspoon baking powder
½	teaspoon salt
1½	cups unsweetened blueberries
1	egg
½	cup milk
½	cup melted margarine

Preheat the oven to 400°. Grease 12 muffin cups. In a medium bowl mix together the flours, sugar, baking powder, and salt. Beat in the egg. Add the milk and margarine. Mix well. Fold in the berries. Pour the batter into the prepared cups. Bake for 20 minutes.

MAKES 12 MUFFINS.

Ronnie Hutchins • The Inspirations

Whispering Hope Banana Macadamia Nut Bread

1 cup butter, softened, or 1 cup oil

2 cups sugar

4 eggs, beaten well

6 to 7 mashed bananas

2½ cups sifted all-purpose flour

1 teaspoon salt

2 teaspoons baking soda

½ cup chopped macadamia nuts

Preheat the oven to 350°. In a large bowl cream the butter or oil and the sugar well. Add the eggs and beat well. Add the mashed bananas and combine well. In a separate bowl sift together the flour, salt, and baking soda. Mix the dry ingredients into the batter. Add the nuts. Do not overmix after adding the dry ingredients and nuts. Bake in 2 large loaf pans or 5 smaller ones for 50 to 60 minutes or until done. For muffins, fill muffin cups three-fourths full and bake for 35 to 45 minutes.

MAKES 2 LOAVES, 5 SMALL LOAVES, OR 12 LARGE MUFFINS.

Jim Nabors

Jim Nabors is well known as the star of 1960s Gomer Pyle, U.S.M.C., *but the man with an incredible voice has recorded more than three dozen albums, including several successful gospel albums. He says his favorite gospel song is "How Great Thou Art."*

Sensational Cinnamon Rolls Up Yonder

Dough:

1   ¼-ounce envelope dry yeast

¼   cup warm water

1   cup scalded milk

¼   cup sugar

¼   cup shortening or butter

1   teaspoon salt

4   cups all-purpose flour

1   egg

Filling:

¼   cup butter, melted

¾   cup firmly packed brown sugar

2   tablespoons ground cinnamon

Icing:

1 16-ounce box confectioners' sugar

¼   cup hot milk

1   teaspoon vanilla extract

Having a good visit are, left to right, Ed Hill (the voice behind "Elvis has left the building"), Clay Harper, J.D. Sumner, Ed Harper, and Jeff Harper.

Dissolve the yeast in the warm water. Combine the hot milk, sugar, shortening, and salt, and let cool to lukewarm. Combine 1½ cups of the flour, the yeast, egg, and warm milk mixture. Then add the remaining flour. Cover the dough and let it rise until double. Roll out the dough in a rectangular shape to ¼-inch thickness.

Preheat the oven to 400°. Spread the melted butter over the rolled out dough. Next, spread the brown sugar over the dough. Sprinkle the cinnamon over the brown sugar. Roll up the dough and filling into a log shape. Slice into ½-inch pieces. Place on a greased cookie sheet very close together, but not touching. Bake for 12 to 15 minutes or until light golden brown.

In a medium bowl combine the confectioners' sugar, milk, and vanilla extract. Spread generously on the warm rolls. Enjoy.

MAKES ABOUT 12.

Karen (Mrs. Clay) Harper • Harper & Associates

Peanut Butter Banana Boat

While on the road, one thing that Brian Free & Assurance do without fail is watch *The Andy Griffith Show*. A fan for years, Brian claims he's probably seen every show and has all but memorized the dialogues. In 1997, viewers of TNN's *Prime Time Country* saw Brian talking about his love of *The Andy Griffith Show*, when he was a surprised by a visit from George Lindsey (Goober)!

It comes as no surprise that Brian's favorite recipe comes straight out of *Aunt Bee's Mayberry Cookbook* (page 94). When not on the road, Brian enjoys these down-home Mayberry recipes with his wife, Pam, and two sons, Ricky and Bryce—recipes that no doubt remind him of some of his favorite episodes! This recipe originates with David Allen of Birmingham, Alabama.

> *Peanut butter to taste*
> 1   *slice bread, preferably whole wheat*
> ½   *banana, peeled*
> 8   *to 12 raisins (optional)*
> 1   *glass cold skim milk (optional)*

Spread the peanut butter on the bread. Place the banana diagonally on the bread and roll up the sides. Top with raisins. Wash down with cold milk.

SERVES 1.

Brian Free

Brian Free & Assurance began in Atlanta, Georgia, in 1994, and scored with top hits immediately, which earned them the Horizon Group of the Year from the Hearts Aflame Awards and The Singing News *Fan Awards in 1995. Among their hits are "Stand Up for What I Stand for," "Mercy Granted One More Time" and "He Thought of Me." Left to right are Bob Caldwell, Randy Crawford, Brian Free, and Jon McBroom.*

Hallelujah Ham and Cheese Sandwiches

My sister wanted to give me her recipes for Florentine Pie and Quiche Lorraine, but I realized that all of my friends who might read this would know that I couldn't possibly make either of these dishes because I find it impossible to properly crack and separate an egg. So instead, I decided to provide you with my specialty, ham and cheese sandwiches.

2   slices bread (my preference is Sunbeam white)

     Mayonnaise (enough to cover adequately both slices of bread; Kraft is the best)

1   slice ham (or more, if you like)

1   slice cheese (or more, if you like)

Evenly spread the mayonnaise on one side of both slices of bread. Place the ham and cheese on top of the mayonnaise on one slice of bread. Top with the other slice of bread, and you have a delicious entrée—three of the basic food groups. Serve this dish with potato chips and four basic food groups have been covered. Of course, I prefer Reduced Fat Ruffles, which help to balance out the extremely high fat grams in the mayonnaise.

MAKES 1 SANDWICH.

Deana Surles • Writer's Ink

SONGWRITERS AND THEIR SONGS
Match the songwriter with his or her Gospel Music Association Song of the Year, plus the year it was awarded the Dove:

1. "The Lighthouse"   A. Kris Kristofferson   aa. 1972
2. "Upon This Rock"   B. Bill Gaither   bb. 1974
3. "We Shall Behold Him"   C. Marijohn Wilkin and Kris Kristofferson   cc. 1973
4. "One Day at a Time"   D. Ron Hinson   dd. 1975
5. "Why Me, Lord?"   E. Gloria Gaither   ee. 1985
6. "Because He Lives"   F. Dottie Rambo   ff. 1982

Answers
1. D, aa; 2. E, ee; 3. F, ff; 4. C, dd; 5. A, cc; 6. B, bb

❧ ENTRÉES ❧

For Goodness Sake Grilled Sirloin

½	cup butter
¼	cup fresh minced parsley
¼	cup minced onion
2	teaspoons Worcestershire sauce
½	teaspoon dry mustard
½	teaspoon coarse ground black pepper
1	to 2 pounds sirloin steak

In a saucepan combine the butter, parsley, onion, Worcestershire sauce, dry mustard, and pepper, and beat until the butter melts. Set aside. Slash the edges of the steak. Broil 3 to 4 inches from the heat for 10 to 12 minutes on each side for rare or 14 to 16 minutes for medium, brushing frequently with the butter mixture. The steak may also be grilled on a gas or charcoal grill.

SERVES 2.

Ina and Jerry Goff

Jerry Goff announces a winner at the 1996 Hearts Aflame Awards.

Top Sirloin Magic

1   top sirloin roast

1   8-ounce bottle Italian salad dressing

1   cup chopped chives

1   cup minced garlic

In a resealable plastic bag combine all of the ingredients and marinate for 1 hour. Charcoal grill the sirloin over indirect heat for 2 hours. Serve and enjoy!

SERVINGS DEPEND ON THE ROAST SIZE AND APPETITES.

Spring Hill Music Group

Cooking up something good in the kitchen of the Spring Hill Music Group, Bill Gaither's record label, are, left to right, Rodney Hatfield, Ray Gibson, Lannie Cates, Scott Chancey, Phil Johnson, and Greg Howard.

Roy's Favorite Pot Roast

3	to 4-pound chuck roast
	Oil
3	potatoes
2	onions
1	12-ounce bag carrots
1	cup water

Place the roast in an aluminum roaster on top of the stove. Put enough oil in the pan to brown the roast on all sides. Brown over medium-high heat. Reduce the heat to medium-low and cook for 1 hour for each pound.

Cut up the vegetables. Add the vegetables and water to the roaster and cook for 40 minutes more on medium high.

SERVES 6 TO 8.

Thaba (Mrs. Roy) Carter • The Chuck Wagon Gang

The Chuck Wagon Gang began in 1935 as one of Southern Gospel's early mixed quartets when D.P. (Dad) Carter and three of his nine children (Rose, Anna, and Jim) formed The Carter Quartet. Performing mostly western tunes, they went on the air on Fort Worth's WBAP radio station and at the request of the sponsor changed their name to that of an earlier group that filled that time slot but which had since disbanded. This new version of the "Chuck Wagon Gang of the Air" became incredibly popular and received tons of fan mail. The group also got more and more requests for gospel songs, and thus they gradually switched to all gospel. On November 25, 1936, they made their first record for Columbia Records ("The Son Hath Made Me Free"). They stuck with Columbia for more than forty years and sold more than 30 million records. When the group made its first personal-appearance tour in 1951, the Gang added two more brothers, Roy and Eddie, and Anna's husband Howard Gordon to the group as Jim and Dad dropped out. The Chuck Wagon Gang of the 1960s included, left to right, Howard Gordon, Roy Carter, Ronnie Page, Louise Clark, and Anna Carter Gordon. Among their crowd pleasers are "I'll Fly Away," "The Church in the Wildwood," "Looking for a City," "I'll Meet You in the Morning," and "He Set Me Free."

Boneless Pot Roast

1	2-pound boneless roast
4	to 6 ribs celery
4	to 6 carrots
6	medium potatoes, quartered
½	medium onion, chopped
1	medium green bell pepper, chopped
	Water
½	teaspoon salt
½	teaspoon black pepper
	Dash red pepper
¼	teaspoon dried basil
¼	teaspoon dried rosemary
¼	teaspoon dried parsley
¼	teaspoon celery seed

In a large electric skillet brown the meat. Drain. Add the vegetables and about 3 cups of water and cook at 350° for about 3 hours.

Add the seasonings about 30 minutes before serving. Add more water as needed.

SERVES 4 TO 6 PEOPLE.

Bobby Goodman • The Happy Goodman Family

Thousands were fed that good ole gospel music when The Happy Goodman Family played on The Gospel Singing Jubilee. *Left to right are Sam, Vestal, Rusty, Bob, and Howard Goodman (on piano), with Dwayne Friend on guitar.*

Take These Burdens Beef Brisket

1	untrimmed whole brisket
	Lemon juice
2	tablespoons Liquid Smoke
¼	cup Worcestershire sauce
	McCormick brand peppered Season-All (or lemon pepper)

An untrimmed brisket will have a heavy pad of fat on the bottom. Trim off as much fat as you wish. I leave about ¼ inch. Also trim off any other large hunks of fat. Place in a 9 x 13-inch (or larger) pan. (I prefer to use glass.) Pour lemon juice over the top of the meat until the meat is standing in juice (about 1 inch high up the side of the pan). Sprinkle the Liquid Smoke and Worcestershire sauce over the meat. Shake the seasoned pepper over the meat until the entire top is well covered. Place foil over the top of the baking dish and marinate in the refrigerator for at least 12 hours.

Bake at 225° for 7 hours. Leave the foil on during baking. I place a cookie sheet with sides under my baking pan to catch the spill-overs. Let cool for at least 1 hour before slicing.

Note: I have marinated mine for up to 24 hours. You can use much smaller brisket pieces, but you will have to experiment with the cooking time.

Janet Paschal

Janet Paschal was a popular member of The Nelons for several years before going solo. With five albums to her credit, she has sold more than a half a million records and has twice been nominated for Dove Awards.

He's Still in the Fire Pepper Steak

2	pounds round steak, cut into strips
	Vegetable oil
1	envelope Lipton onion soup mix
	Water
	Cornstarch
1	large green bell pepper, cut into strips

In a deep skillet brown the steak in a small amount of oil. Sprinkle the soup mix over the steak. Add water to almost cover the steak and cook until tender. Thicken with cornstarch. Add the pepper and cook until tender. Serve over rice.

SERVES 6.

Brock Speer • The Speers

Brock Speer accepts the 1996 SGMG Heritage Award from Ed Harper and Randy Owen of the country music vocal band Alabama.

The Speers

Known as "America's First Family of Gospel Music," The Speers began in 1921 when G.T. "Dad" Speer, a Georgia farmboy turned music teacher, formed the first Speer Quartet in Double Springs, Alabama. The group consisted of Dad, his wife Lena, who played the piano, and his sister and brother-in-law, Pearl and Logan Claborn, at a time when the field was dominated by all-male quartets.

When the Claborns departed the group in 1925, the children (Brock, Rosa Nell, Mary Tom, and Ben) began filling in and before long it literally was The Speer Family. It was also that same year that the group began traveling to singing conventions and other appearances via automobile, a new model T Ford, rather than the ol' two-horse wagon.

Many fine singers have been a part of The Speers throughout the years, including favorites Jeanne Johnson and Sue Chenault Dodge as well as Mom and Dad Speer's grandchildren Steve, Darin, Mark, and Susan. Time has brought the group full circle now with Rosa Nell, Mary Tom, Ben, Brock, and Faye making up The Speers.

The Speers have won eight Dove awards for best mixed group of the year, two Dove awards for best album, and four Dove awards for best female vocalist. Seven times the group has been nominated for Grammy awards. Dad, Mom, Brock, and Ben are all members of the Gospel Music Hall of Fame.

The Speers, the longest-running group in gospel music, have recorded more than seventy albums in their seventy-seven years. Among their

The Speers pose with Tennessee Governor Don Sundquist after being honored by the State of Tennessee for their seventy-five years of singing. From left to right are Homeland Records chief executive Bill Traylor, Rosa Nell Speer, Governor Sundquist, Mary Tom Reid, and Ben Speer.

most requested tunes are "City Coming Down," "In the Midst of It All," "Interceding," "The Dearest Friend I Ever Had," "The King Is Coming," "Heaven's Jubilee," "He's Still in the Fire," and "Saved to the Uttermost."

The thread running true through all the years is Dad Speer's simple philosophy: "Always sing what you feel and feel what you sing."

Excuses Pepper Steak

1½   *pounds round steak (1 inch thick), cut into strips*

      All-purpose flour

¼   *cup oil*

      Salt and pepper to taste

1¾   *cups water*

1   *10-ounce can Ro-tel tomatoes, drained and liquid reserved*

½   *cup onions, chopped*

1½   *tablespoons Worcestershire sauce*

2   *green bell peppers, diced*

      Rice, cooked

Dredge the steak strips in flour. In a skillet heat the oil. Season the steak with salt and pepper and brown in the hot oil. Add the water, liquid from the tomatoes, and onions. Cover and simmer for 1 hour and 15 minutes.

Uncover and stir in the Worcestershire sauce, tomatoes, and peppers. Simmer for 5 minutes. Serve over hot rice.

SERVES 6 TO 8.

Raydean Reese • The Kingsmen

The history of the Kingsmen goes back to 1956. Since then the group has had fourteen Number One songs, including "Excuses," the longest-running Number One song in gospel history (nineteen consecutive months in 1981 and 1982). Standing, from left to right, are Parker Jonathan, Rory Rigdon, Randy Miller, Chris Collins, and Bryan Hutson. Seated, from left to right, are Greg Fox, Eldridge Fox, Andrew Ishee, and Raydean Reese.

Something Better than Gold Pepper Steak and Rice

3	cups hot cooked rice
1	pound lean beef (round steak) cut ½ inch thick
1	tablespoon paprika
2	tablespoons butter
2	cloves garlic, crushed
1½	cups beef broth
2	tablespoons cornstarch
¼	cup water
¼	cup soy sauce
1	cup sliced green onions, including tops
2	green bell peppers, cut into strips
2	large green tomatoes, cut into eighths

While the rice is cooking, pound the steak into ¼-inch thickness. Cut into ¼-inch-wide strips. Sprinkle the meat with paprika and allow the meat to stand while preparing the other ingredients.

In a large skillet brown the meat in the butter. Add the garlic and broth. Cover and simmer for 30 minutes.

In a separate bowl blend the cornstarch, water, and soy sauce. Stir the onions and green peppers into the meat and simmer for another 5 minutes. Stir the cornstarch mixture into the meat sauce. Cook, stirring until clear and thickened, about 2 minutes. Add the tomatoes and stir gently. Serve over rice.

SERVES 4.

Dixie McKeithen • The McKeithens

Poor Man's Steak

1½ pounds lean ground beef

½ cup chopped onion

½ cup milk

½ teaspoon salt

½ cup saltine cracker crumbs

  All-purpose flour

  Vegetable cooking spray

1 10¾-ounce can cream of mushroom soup

In a large bowl combine the ground beef, onion, milk, salt, and cracker crumbs. Pat the mixture on a cookie sheet and refrigerate overnight.

  Cut into 6 squares. Dredge each square in the flour and brown in a large skillet coated with vegetable spray. Place in a 9 x 13-inch baking pan. Cover with mushroom soup. Bake at 350° for 40 to 50 minutes.

SERVES 6.

Janis Lewis Phillips • The Lewis Family

I'll Sail Away Home Steak

  Cubed steak

  Salt and pepper

  All-purpose flour

  Vegetable oil

Salt and pepper the steak and then dredge it in flour. Fry the steak in a small amount of vegetable oil just long enough to brown it. Place the steak in a baking dish and cover it with foil. Bake at 350° for 1 hour.

Haskell Cooley and Family • The Cooleys

Chime In Chicken Fried Steak with Tomato Gravy

2   pounds cubed steak, cut into serving sizes
    Salt
    Pepper
    Vegetable oil
    All-purpose flour
    Garlic powder (optional)
1   14½-ounce can stewed tomatoes
    Milk

Sprinkle both sides of the steak with salt and pepper. Coat each side with flour. Pour enough oil in a frying pan to cover the bottom and heat to medium. Place the steak in the pan, cover with a lid, fry, and brown both sides of the steak. Remove from the pan and drain on paper towels.

To the pan drippings from the steak add enough flour to make a roux. Brown, stirring constantly. Add salt, pepper, and garlic powder to taste and brown until chocolate in color. Add the stewed tomatoes and enough milk to make the desired thickness of gravy. Continue cooking over medium heat until thickened. (If the gravy becomes too thick, add a little more milk and stir.) You may add the fried steak to the gravy and heat for about 10 minutes. Serve over rice.

SERVES 3 TO 4.

Mr. and Mrs. Les Beasley

Les Beasley (right) with animal expert Jack Hanna following their appearances on a taping of The Nashville Network's Prime Time Country.

ANNUAL SOUTHERN GOSPEL SINGING CONVENTIONS

JANUARY

T & T Promotions Annual New Year's Sing, Spartanburg, SC

Annual Melbourne Gospel Jubilee, Melbourne Auditorium, Melbourne, FL

Mid-Winter Gospel Jubilee, GA Mountain Center, Gainesville, GA

Jubilee at Sea Cruise, Bahamas

Anniversary Celebration Gospel Sing Weekend, Church of God State Arena, Wimauma, FL

FEBRUARY

Annual Gospel Fest, Crossroads Baptist Church, Highland City, FL

Annual Gospel Sing, Westfall High School, Westfall, OH

MARCH

Mashburns Anniversary Concert, St. Clair County High School, Odenville, AL

Spring Gospel Singing, Tugham High School, Paducah, KY

Annual Southern Gospel Music Concert, Jamil Shrine Temple, Columbia, SC

Annual Meramec Caverns Easter Sing, Meramec Caverns, Stanton, MO

APRIL

Primitive's Anniversary Sing, Georgia Mountain Center, Gainesville, GA

Annual Garden Spot Anniversary Singing, Mennonite High School, Lancaster, PA

Florida Gospel Music Spring Jamboree, Dixieland Music Park, Waldo, FL

East Tennessee Gospel Jamboree, Viking Hall Civic Center, Bristol, TN

Roy Knight Singers Anniversary, Anderson Civic Center, Anderson, SC

Inspirations' Anniversary Sing, Cobb Civic Center, Marietta, GA

Annual Singfest, Oral Roberts University, Mabee Center, Tulsa, OK

MAY

Great Western Quartet Convention, Selland Arena, Fresno, CA

Garden Spot Promotions Annual Cathedrals Concert, Mennonite High School, Lancaster, PA

Southern Gospel Music Association Hall of Fame Induction Ceremony, Pigeon Forge, TN

Memorial Weekend Gospel Sing, Landisville Campmeeting Grounds, Landisville, PA

Bill Gaither Family Fest, Gatlinburg Convention Center, Gatlinburg, TN

Dominion Valley Gospel Singing, Dominion Valley Park, Stuart, VA

JUNE

Singing in the Sun, Fairgrounds, Orlando, FL

Singing at Sea Cruise, Bahamas

Suwannee River Jubilee, Spirit of the Suwannee Music Park, Live Oak, FL

Biggest Weekend Gospel Sing, Riverdale High School, Fort Myers, FL

Annual Cathedrals Concert, Georgia Mountain Center, Gainesville, GA

Annual Amish Country Jubilee, Alpine Hills Resort, Sugarcreek, OH

Garden Spot Promotions Annual Summer Sing, Mennonite High School, Lancaster, PA

Annual Singing on the Mountain, Grandfather Mountain, Linville, NC

Buckey's Outdoor Singing Jubilee, Gospel Center Pavilion, Canton, OH

Annual Singing in Hominy Valley, Hominy Valley Music Park, Candler, NC

Annual Waycross All-Night Sing, Memorial Stadium, Waycross, GA

Inspirations' Annual Singing in the Smokies, Inspiration Park, Bryson City, NC

Singing on the Amish Farm, Amish Farm Tourist Complex, Berlin, OH

JULY

Annual Bonifay All-Night Sing, Memorial Field, Bonifay, FL

Bishop's Anniversary Singing, Indian Fort Theater, Berea, KY

Anniversary Singing Echoes Blue Springs Valley Sing, Blue Springs Valley Park, Cleveland, TN

Annual Volunteer State Songfest, Jackson Civic Center, Jackson, TN

Hendersons' Anniversary Concert, Milton High School, Milton, FL

Hopper's North Carolina Singing Convention & Campmeeting, Watermelon Park, Berryville, VA

Gold City Annual Homecoming, Gadsden Convention Hall, Gadsden, Ala. Grand Ole Gospel Reunion, Palmetto Expo Center, Greenville, SC

AUGUST

Annual Albert E. Brumley Sun-Down to Sun-Up Sing, Parsons Rodeo Arena, Springdale, AR

The Greenes' Annual Singing Jubilee, High Country Fairgrounds, Boone, NC

Singing News Annual Open House, Boone, NC

Annual Seminole Sing, City Park, Seminole, OK

Southern Song, Paramount's Carowinds, Charlotte, NC

Garden Spot Promotions Blue Mountain Gospel Music Festival, Community Grounds, Kempton, PA

Singing in the Foothills, Echo Valley, Cleveland, SC

Dominion Valley Gospel Singing, Dominion Valley Park, Stuart, VA

Inspirations' Labor Day Festival, Inspiration Park, Bryson City, NC

SEPTEMBER

Jordan's Annual Gospel Sing, Vanceburg, KY

Annual Greenland Gospel Sing, Appalachian Fairgrounds, Gray, TN

National Quartet Convention, Kentucky Fair & Expo Center, Louisville, KY

Singing News Riverboat Cruise, OH River aboard Belle of Louisville, Louisville, KY

Singing News Fan Awards, Kentucky Fair & Expo Center, Louisville, KY

OCTOBER

Suwannee River Fall Festival, Spirit of the Suwannee Music Park, Live Oak, FL

Southern Gospel Jubilee, Dollywood, Pigeon Forge, TN

Jimmie Davis' Annual Homecoming, Jimmie Davis Tabernacle, Jonesboro, LA

Bill Gaither's Praise Gathering, Convention Center, Indianapolis, IN

Hominy Valley Fall Colors Sing, Hominy Valley Music Park, Candler, NC

Annual Meramec Caverns Sing, Meramec Caverns, Stanton, MO

Singing in the Smokies Fall Color Festival, Inspiration Park, Bryson City, NC

NOVEMBER

Serve the Lord Concert, Winston-Salem, NC

Garden Spot Promotions Annual Fall Concert, Mennonite High School, Lancaster, PA

Spencers' Annual Fall Harvest Concert, Dover High School, Dover, OH

Jerry Foster's Annual Thanksgiving Night, Lee College Conn Center, Cleveland, TN

Annual Thanksgiving Sing, Georgia Mountain Center, Gainesville, GA

Hoppers Annual Homecoming Anniversary Sing, Morehead Senior High School, Eden, NC

DECEMBER

Garden Spot Promotions Annual Bluegrass Christmas, Mennonite High School, Lancaster, PA

Annual New Year's Eve Sings, Georgia Mountain Center, Gainesville, GA

Annual Jubilee Celebration, Charlotte Coliseum, Charlotte, NC

Garden Spot Promotions New Year's Eve Celebration, Cornerstone Christian Supper Club, Lancaster, PA

The Mother of All New Year's Eve Sings, Charleston Municipal Auditorium, Charleston, WV

Resource: *The Music Men, The Story of Professional Gospel Quartet Singing* by Bob Terrell, 55 Dillingham Road, Asheville, N.C. 28805, $19.95 plus postage and handling.

Brashear Bierox

1   *package hot roll mix or other yeast dough*

2   *pounds ground beef*

2   *pounds chopped cabbage*

2   *large onions, chopped*

½   *teaspoon salt*

½   *teaspoon pepper*

½   *teaspoon garlic salt*

Mix the dough according to the package directions and set aside. In a large saucepan, combine the remaining ingredients and cook over medium heat until the ground beef is brown. Drain off the liquid. Roll the dough to ¼-inch thickness. Cut the dough into 5- or 6-inch squares. Place several spoonfuls of the beef mixture into each square. Fold up the edges of the dough and seal the edges. Place upside down on a greased cookie sheet and let rise for 20 to 30 minutes. Bake at 350° for 20 minutes. Serve with salad or a vegetable.

SERVES 6 TO 8.

The Brashear Family

Carry On Cheeseburger Casserole

A kid favorite!

1	pound hamburger
1	small onion, chopped (optional)
6	ounces tomato sauce
¼	cup ketchup
	Salt and pepper to taste
	American cheese slices
1	10-count can refrigerator biscuits (non-flaky)

In a skillet brown the hamburger meat with the onion, and drain. Spread over the bottom of a 9 x 13-inch casserole dish. Mix the tomato sauce, ketchup, and salt and pepper, and then spread over the hamburger. Cover the ketchup mixture with the cheese slices and then cover the cheese with the biscuits. Bake at 350° until the biscuits are golden brown.

SERVES 6.

Beverly and Lynn Fox • The Fox Brothers

The Fox Brothers have been making sweet gospel harmonies since the early 1970s when Lynn, Roy, and Randy sang at a small country church in Bending Chestnut, Tennessee. They've since gone on to become one of the best-known gospel groups out of Middle Tennessee with numerous awards from The Gospel Voice, The Music City News, *and* Cash Box *magazine—including the Number One song of 1993 in both* The Music City News *and* The Gospel Voice *with "Mama's Daily Bread." Among their other top hits are "Each Step I Take," "It's Time for Love," "Carry On," "Somebody To Believe In," and "Don't Look Back." The brothers also host a free, two-night gospel music concert each summer, which draws thousands to their home community. Seen here are, left to right, Lynn Fox, Derrick Conner, Roy Fox, Randy Fox, Marty Lyon, and Erik Foster.*

Sweet Sounds Sweet and Sour Beef and Cabbage

1½ pounds ground beef

½ cup chopped onion

½ cup sliced celery

½ cup chopped green bell pepper

2 tablespoons quick-cooking rolled oats

2 tablespoons snipped parsley

¾ teaspoon salt

¼ teaspoon garlic powder

⅛ teaspoon ground black pepper

1 medium head cabbage

1 15-ounce can tomato sauce

¼ cup cider vinegar

3 tablespoons firmly packed brown sugar

½ teaspoon salt

   Dash pepper

HeavenBound, clockwise from bottom left, Ken Eubanks, Jeff Gibson, Rick Busby, and Lawrence Taylor, began in 1976 when three of the original four members were in college together at Atlantic Christian College. Their career took off in 1982 when their huge hit "Canaanland Is Just in Sight" stayed on the charts for 23 months. One of their more recent hits is "Can the World See Jesus in You."

In a skillet cook the beef, onion, celery, and green pepper until the meat is browned. Drain off the excess fat. Sprinkle the meat mixture with the oats, parsley, ¾ teaspoon of salt, garlic powder, and ⅛ teaspoon of pepper. Core the cabbage and cut it into 6 wedges. Place the cabbage atop the meat.

In a medium bowl combine the tomato sauce, vinegar, brown sugar, ½ teaspoon salt, and a dash of pepper. Mix well. Pour the tomato sauce mixture over the cabbage and meat. Cover and simmer for 15 to 20 minutes or until the cabbage is tender.

MAKES 6 SERVINGS.

HeavenBound

Great Stridings Hamburger Stroganoff

3	tablespoons margarine
2	pounds ground beef
	Salt and pepper to taste
1	15-ounce can tomato sauce
1	8 ounce package medium-wide noodles (½ to ¾ inch)
1	cup chopped onion
1	16-ounce container cottage cheese
8	ounces sour cream
½	teaspoon garlic salt
1	teaspoon Season-All salt
1	cup grated American cheese

In a skillet melt the margarine and brown the ground beef. Add salt, pepper, and tomato sauce and simmer for about 10 minutes.

Cook the noodles as directed on the package. When tender, drain and add the onion, cottage cheese, sour cream, salt, pepper to taste, garlic salt, and Season-All. Mix thoroughly. In a large Pyrex dish alternate layers of noodle mixture and beef mixture and top with the grated cheese. Bake at 325° for 45 minutes. Remove the cover for the last 10 minutes of baking time.

SERVES 8.

Elaine Wilburn • The Wilburns

Visiting back stage at the 1995 Hearts Aflame Awards are, left to right, SGMA executive director Heather Campbell, Elaine Wilburn, and Carroll Robertson.

Spanish Beef Wedges

2	pounds ground beef
1	1¼-ounce package taco seasoning
1	egg
1	cup crushed corn chips
1	8-ounce can tomato sauce
	Salt and pepper to taste
	Grated cheese
	Lettuce
	Tomatoes, sliced
	Avocados, cut into wedges
	Onions, sliced (optional)
	Bell peppers, sliced (optional)

In a large bowl combine the beef, taco seasoning, egg, corn chips, tomato sauce, salt, and pepper, and mix well. Transfer to a round cake pan. Bake at 350° for 50 minutes.

Remove the pan from the oven and top with grated cheese. After allowing a few minutes for the cheese to melt, cut into pie-shaped wedges and place in a circle on a serving plate with the lettuce, tomato, and avocado wedges. Top with onion rings and bell pepper rings, if desired.

SERVES 5 TO 6.

Danny Funderburk

Danny Funderburk, formerly of The Cathedrals

Bountiful Beef and Biscuit Casserole

1	8-ounce can biscuits
1	pound ground beef
⅓	cup chopped onions
¼	cup diced green peppers
1	8-ounce can tomato sauce
2	teaspoons chili powder
½	teaspoon garlic salt
1½	cups grated Cheddar cheese
½	cup sour cream
1	egg, slightly beaten

In a skillet brown the beef. Add the onions and peppers, and cook until tender. Drain off the excess fat. Stir in the tomato sauce, chili powder, and garlic salt. Simmer.

Separate the biscuits and pull each biscuit into 2 layers. Press half of the layers into an 8- or 9-inch round casserole dish. In a medium bowl combine half of the cheese, the sour cream, and the egg. Mix. Remove the meat mixture from the heat and stir in the cheese and sour cream mixture. Spoon over the dough. Place the reserved dough on top and sprinkle with the remaining cheese. Bake at 375° for 25 to 30 minutes.

SERVES 4 TO 6.

Debra Talley • The Talley Trio

The original Talleys of Morristown, Tennessee, were among Southern Gospel's favorite trios after they formed in 1984. Previously Debra and Roger sang with The Hoppers and Kirk performed with The Cathedrals. Left to right are Kirk, Debra, and Roger Talley. Among their most well-known songs are "He Is Here," "Sweeter as the Days Go By" and "Triumphantly the Church Will Rise."

Sunset Baked Enchilada Casserole

1	pound ground beef
1	medium onion, chopped
1	10¾-ounce can cream of mushroom soup
½	cup chopped green chilies
1	14-ounce can taco sauce
½	cup hot sauce
1	cup evaporated milk
12	corn tortillas, cut into quarters
1	pound Cheddar cheese, grated

In a skillet cook the ground beef and onion until the meat is crumbly, but not brown. Add the soups, chilies, taco sauce, hot sauce, and milk. Cook over medium heat, stirring constantly, until bubbly. In a rectangular baking dish make layers of tortillas, beef mixture, and cheese. Repeat the layers, ending with cheese. Bake at 325° for 40 to 45 minutes.

SERVES 8.

Henry Slaughter

Arise Spanish Delight

1	pound lean ground beef
1	8-ounce package egg noodles
1	onion, chopped
1	green bell pepper, chopped
1	15-ounce can cream-style corn
1	10¾-ounce can tomato soup
½	soup can water
	Grated cheese

In a skillet brown the ground beef, onion, and bell pepper. In a medium bowl combine the corn, soup, and water. Add the corn mixture to the beef. Simmer for about 15 minutes.

Boil and drain the noodles. Layer the noodles, beef mixture, and cheese in a rectangular baking dish. Bake at 375° for about 15 minutes or until bubbly and the cheese has melted.

SERVES 4 TO 6.

Connie Fortner • The McKameys

The McKameys, based in Clinton, Tennessee, have seven Number One songs including "God on the Mountain," "Arise," and "Who Put the Tears in the Eyes of the Lamb." Since they became a full-time group in 1980, they've recorded seventeen albums. Peg is noted for kicking off her shoes and dancing across the stage when the spirit leads. Clockwise from bottom left are Peg McKamey Bean, Carol Woodard, Ruben Bean, and Connie Fortner.

Let Us Gather at the River Lasagna

1	pound ground beef
½	cup chopped onion
1	garlic clove, crushed
2	tablespoons chopped parsley
1	teaspoon dried basil leaves
1	16-ounce can finely chopped tomatoes
1	15-ounce can tomato sauce
12	uncooked lasagna noodles (about 12 ounces)
1	pint ricotta cheese or creamed cottage cheese
½	cup grated Parmesan cheese
1	cup grated mozzarella cheese
1	tablespoon chopped fresh parsley

In a large skillet cook the ground beef, onion, and garlic, stirring occasionally, until the beef is brown. Drain. Stir in the 2 tablespoons of parsley, basil, tomatoes, and tomato sauce. Heat to boiling, stirring occasionally. Reduce the heat and simmer uncovered for about 45 minutes or until slightly thickened.

Preheat the oven to 350°. In a large pot cook the lasagna noodles as directed on the package. Drain. In a medium bowl mix the ricotta cheese, ¼ cup of Parmesan cheese, ⅔ cup of mozzarella, and 1 tablespoon of parsley. Spread a thin layer of sauce in a greased 9 x 13-inch baking dish. Top with 4 noodles, then 1 cup of cheese mixture, and then 1 cup more sauce. Repeat with 2 more layers, ending with sauce. Top with the remaining ⅓ cup of mozzarella cheese and ¼ cup of Parmesan cheese. Cover with foil and bake for 30 minutes. Uncover and bake 15 minutes longer or until hot and bubbly. Let stand before cutting.

SERVES 8.

Deana Surles • Writer's Ink

Lazy Day Easy Lasagna

I can remember when I was a growing boy that our day always ended with the family gathering on the front porch and talking, singing, and just relaxing as we settled in for the night. Some of those days were hectic and fast-paced, while others were more calm and, well, lazy. I liked those lazy days. But I found that they don't last forever. Responsibilities and cares gradually replace the carefree days of youth. But we can relive those days with a dish from the past.

6   to 8 lasagna noodles

1   pound ground beef

1   14-ounce jar Ragu tomato sauce

2   cups grated mozzarella cheese

In a large pot boil the lasagna noodles until done. In a skillet brown the ground beef and drain the grease. Pour the tomato sauce into the pan with the meat and cook until heated through.

   Butter a 9 x 13-inch pan and place a layer of the noodles on the bottom. Cover with a layer of the meat mixture. Repeat the layers. Cover with mozzarella cheese. Bake at 350° until the cheese is melted.

SERVES 4.

Kenny Bishop • The Bishops

Kenny Bishop (center) visits with Ed Harper (left) and Singing News *publisher Jerry Kirksey at the 1996 Opryland Gospel Jubilee, sponsored by* The Singing News.

The Bishops

It was a tape recording for their beloved grandmother that saw the humble beginnings of The Bishops in 1984. The trio had gone into the RCM studios in Winchester, Kentucky, and laid down their harmonies for the first time on a record. They took a copy of that first record to their Granny Bishop's house in Berea, Kentucky, and have since gone on to become one of the top Southern Gospel trios.

Natives of Waco, Kentucky, The Bishops is composed of two brothers, lead vocalist Mark Bishop and tenor Kenny Bishop, and their father, baritone Kenneth Bishop. Musically they are assisted by acoustic guitarist Carl Williams Jr., who also rings in with the group vocally when they share their "front porch singing," the Bishops' trademark.

"Growing up, we used to go out on the front porch in the early evenings and sit around and sing," says Mark. "We didn't have any instruments, we just sang. That's really how we got started, so it only seems fitting that we share that style of music with our audiences."

Being from Eastern Kentucky, the threesome's musical style in the early days had more of a bluegrass flavor than their current sound which is much more diversified.

"People really don't know what to call us. We're just a male trio singing gospel music," says Kenny. "Individually, we enjoy various types of music. I think that style variation comes through on our recordings and in concert."

Kenneth is the group's founder and leader and has enjoyed singing with his two sons for more than fourteen years. He and wife Shirley Bishop have two other sons, Loren and Chris.

Mark is not only the lead vocalist of The Bishops but he is one of Southern Gospel's most prolific songwriters. Residing in Possum Run, Kentucky, he once served unofficially as the town's mayor.

The Bishops began their career after entering a small studio in order to make a recording of their songs for their Granny Bishop in Berea, Kentucky. Left to right are Kenny, Kenneth, and Mark Bishop.

Kenny's longtime dream was to be involved in full-time musical ministry. He is an ordained minister and holds revivals across the United States when the group is not performing.

Bass player/vocalist Carl Williams Jr. originally joined the Bishops in 1985 but left in 1989. He re-enlisted with the group in 1996.

The Homeland Records artists have had numerous hit songs, including the Number One tunes "He's in the Midst," "He's My Hiding Place," and "You Can't Ask Too Much of My God." The Bishops have also won various awards throughout the 1990s. They were the *Gospel Voice* Diamond Voice Male Trio of the Year in 1991 and 1994, won the Heart's Aflame Award Concert Video of the Year in 1995, and were a *Singing News* Fan Award Favorite Group Top 10 Nominee from 1991 to 1995.

Si the Light Mexican Casserole

As always, I was on another one of my diets. I spent $350 to join Nutri-Systems and was bound and determined to stick with it. I went to Pennsylvania to do a concert. The church there heard about my love for Mexican food, and they did a potluck dinner for me—with every dish being Mexican! It was only by the Grace of God and the memory of the $350 diet program fee that I kept from eating any of it at all.

1   pound ground beef

1   pound Velveeta cheese, cubed

1   10¾-ounce can cream of mushroom soup

1   10¾-ounce can cream of chicken soup

1   14-ounce can mild enchilada sauce

1   package tortillas (corn or flour)

In a large skillet brown the meat. Drain. Mix ¾ of the Velveeta into the meat and stir until melted. Add the soups and enchilada sauce. Cut the tortillas into small pieces and add to the mixture. Heat for a short while. Pour the mixture into an ovenproof pan. Spread the remaining cheese over the mixture and bake at 350° until the cheese on top has melted.

SERVES 6.

Barbara Fairchild

Country music star Barbara Fairchild entered gospel music via the group Heirloom, alongside Candy Hemphill-Christmas and Tonya Goodman Sykes. Today she is a solo performer and operates The Barbara Fairchild Theater in Branson, Missouri.

Tell It on the Mountain Taco Casserole

1	7-ounce package Doritos
1½	pounds ground beef
	Salt and pepper to taste
¼	cup minced onion
1	10¾-ounce can cream of chicken soup
1	10¾-ounce can cream of mushroom soup
1	10-ounce can Ro-tel tomatoes
	Sliced American cheese

Place the Doritos in the bottom of a 9 x 13-inch baking dish. In a skillet brown the meat and season to taste. Drain the excess fat and then sprinkle the meat over the chips. Place the onions evenly on top of the meat.

In a saucepan heat the soups and tomatoes until bubbly. Pour over the casserole. Cover with slices of cheese. Bake at 400° until the cheese is melted. Serve hot.

Note: If you don't like it too spicy, only add half of a can of Ro-tel.

SERVES 6.

Jay Parrack • Gold City Quartet

Hey Jay, is somebody raiding the icebox?

Mr. and Mrs. Jay Parrack at home.

Masterful Meat Loaf

1	pound ground chuck
1	large onion, chopped
1	green bell pepper, diced
1	cup crushed saltines
½	cup ketchup
1	tablespoon A-1 steak sauce
1	tablespoon Worcestershire sauce
½	teaspoon cayenne pepper
¼	teaspoon minced garlic
1	10¾-ounce can tomato soup
6	slices Swiss cheese

In a large bowl mix the beef, onion, bell pepper, saltines, ketchup, A-1 sauce, Worcestershire sauce, cayenne pepper, and garlic. Form the mixture into 6 small loaves. In a skillet brown the tops and bottoms of the loaves over medium heat. Pour the tomato soup over the loaves, reduce heat to low, and cook for 30 minutes. Put 1 slice of cheese on each loaf, cover, and heat for 5 minutes.

MAKES 6 LOAVES.
The Rhythm Masters

Norman's Revolutionary Stuffed Meat Loaf

Meat Loaf:

1½	pounds ground beef
½	pound ground pork
4	slices bread, soaked in milk and drained
1	onion, finely chopped
1	tablespoon salt
½	teaspoon pepper
2	eggs

Stuffing:

¼   cup (½ stick) butter

3   onions, finely chopped

2   ribs celery, finely chopped

1½   cups bread crumbs

½   teaspoon sage

½   teaspoon salt

⅛   teaspoon pepper

2   tablespoons parsley

2   tablespoons water

1   egg, well beaten

Topping:

2   tablespoons melted butter

½   cup water

½   cup chili sauce

Daywind's A&R director Norman Holland, second from left, celebrates the launch of the When Men Pray *project at the 1996 National Quartet Convention in Louisville, Kentucky, with Daywind Music Group president Dottie Leonard Miller, The Gaither Vocal Band's Mark Lowry (who also is a lead vocalist for* When Men Pray), *and Brenda McClain.*

In a large bowl combine the beef, pork, bread, onion, salt, pepper, and eggs, and thoroughly blend. Use ⅔ of the mixture to line the bottom and sides of a loaf pan. Set aside.

In a cast-iron skillet melt the butter. Add the onion and celery and fry until the onions are translucent. Stir in the remaining ingredients and sauté until lightly browned. Remove from the stove and stir in the beaten egg. Fill the center portion of the meat-covered loaf pan with the stuffing. Cover the stuffing with the remaining meat mixture.

Spread the top of the loaf with the melted butter. Pour the water over this and cover with chili sauce. Bake in a 350° oven for 45 minutes.

SERVES 6 TO 8.

Norman Holland • Daywind Music Group

Statesmen Sweet and Sour Meatballs

2   pounds ground beef (ground round is best)

1   cup finely crushed corn flakes,

⅓   cup parsley flakes

2   eggs, beaten

2   tablespoons soy sauce

¼   teaspoon ground black pepper

½   teaspoon garlic powder

2   tablespoons minced onion

⅓   cup ketchup

Sauce:

1   16-ounce can cranberry sauce (smooth, not whole berry)

1   12-ounce bottle chili sauce

2   tablespoons brown sugar

1   tablespoon lemon juice

In a large bowl combine the ground beef, corn flakes, parsley, eggs, soy sauce, pepper, garlic powder, minced onion, and ketchup. Blend together and roll into balls about the size of silver dollars. Place in a rectangular baking dish.

In a medium bowl mix together the cranberry sauce, chili sauce, brown sugar, and lemon juice. Pour the mixture over the meatballs. Bake at 350° for 30 to 45 minutes.

SERVES ABOUT 8.

Gail (Mrs. Jack) Toney • The Statesmen

Beefy Mushroom-Stuffed Manicotti Medlock

1	pound ground beef
1	cup sliced fresh mushrooms
½	cup chopped onion
½	cup chopped green bell pepper
½	teaspoon salt
1	32-ounce jar spaghetti sauce
1	16-ounce package ribbed manicotti noodles, cooked
½	cup fresh grated Parmesan cheese

In a large skillet brown the ground beef. Drain. Add the mushrooms, onion, green pepper, and salt. Cook until the onions are translucent. Add ¾ cup of the spaghetti sauce and mix well.

Pour a small amount of spaghetti sauce in the bottom of a 2-quart casserole dish. Fill the manicotti with the meat mixture and place in the dish. Spoon the remaining spaghetti sauce over the manicotti. Cover and bake at 350° for 25 to 30 minutes. Remove the cover and sprinkle the Parmesan cheese over top. Return to oven for 5 minutes.

SERVES 6.

Rhonda Medlock • The Medlocks

Hear the Sound Chicken Spaghetti

½   cup (1 stick) butter of margarine

⅓   cup chopped onions

½   cup chopped celery

1   10¾-ounce can cream of mushroom soup

1   10-ounce can Ro-tel tomatoes

1   whole chicken, boiled, boned, and chopped

1   12-ounce package spaghetti noodles, cooked

     Grated cheese

In a saucepan melt the butter and sauté the onions and celery until tender. Add the soup and tomatoes and cook for 10 minutes. Add the chopped chicken and the spaghetti. Transfer the mixture to a 9 x 13-inch pan and top with grated cheese. Bake at 350° for 30 minutes.

SERVES 6.

The Dixie Echoes

The Dixie Echoes, left to right, Dale Shelnut, Larry Ford, Joe Whitfield, Sue Whitfield, Randy Shelnut, and Ken Turner, was begun by promoter J.G. Whitfield with his brother Joe and Joe's wife, Sue. It was with this group that Jack Toney began his career as one of the all-time great lead singers. He was replaced by Alabaman Dale Shelnut, one of the best ever at black spirituals.

Common Bond Chicken Spaghetti

We are chicken and pasta lovers. This is one of our favorite dishes and satisfies our taste for both.

4	to 6 chicken breasts
1	quart water
1	whole yellow or white onion
½	green bell pepper
	Salt and pepper to taste
12	ounces spaghetti noodles
1	10¾-ounce can cream of mushroom soup
1	10-ounce can stewed tomatoes (picante sauce may be substituted)
1	cup grated Cheddar cheese

In a large saucepan boil the chicken until tender in the water with the onion, green pepper, and salt and pepper. Remove the chicken and set aside to cool. Remove the onion and pepper from the broth and then boil the spaghetti in the chicken broth. (You may need to add extra water or broth.) Drain the spaghetti. In the pot with the drained spaghetti add the mushroom soup, stewed tomatoes, and most of the grated cheese. Bone the chicken and cut into cubes. Add the chicken to the noodle mixture. Place the mixture in a casserole dish, top with cheese, and bake at 350° until bubbly.

SERVES 4 TO 6.

Common Bond

The trio Common Bond is composed of Mark, Luke, and John Green, the only group of identical triplets in Christian music. The Florida natives first performed together at the age of five and upon graduation from high school all three were awarded full college scholarships. Among their hits are "Tower of Power" and "Favor My Saviour." Left to right are John, Mark, and Luke.

Chicken Melanzana with Spaghetti

No side dishes are necessary except for a salad.

2	whole large chicken breasts (1½ pound total), split
	Garlic salt
	Freshly ground pepper
1	small eggplant (¾ pound), peeled and cubed
½	cup chopped onion
1	6-ounce can tomato paste
1	cup water
½	teaspoon Italian seasoning
3	cups tender-cooked spaghetti

Season the chicken pieces with garlic salt and pepper and place them skin side up in a shallow roasting pan. Quick-bake at 450° for 15 to 20 minutes until well-browned. Pour off all the fat.

In a medium bowl combine the eggplant, onion, tomato paste, water, and Italian seasoning, and pour it around the chicken. Cover the roaster loosely with foil and bake at 350° for 40 to 50 minutes, stirring occasionally, until the chicken is tender and the liquid is reduced to a thick sauce.

Serve with ¾ cup of spaghetti per person.

SERVES 4.

Bernadette and Terry Bradshaw

Former Pittsburgh Steeler quarterback great Terry Bradshaw toured as a gospel singer for three years and has had two top-selling gospel albums, Until You *and* Here in My Heart, *which were both nominated for Dove Awards. In 1996 he released his album with Jake Hess titled* Terry & Jake.

Fly Away Chicken Spaghetti Casserole

2   chickens, boiled and boned to yield 3 to 4 cups of cooked meat, reserving broth
      Water

1   12-ounce package spaghetti
      Salt and pepper to taste

1   stick margarine, melted

1   onion, finely chopped

1   green pepper, chopped

1   2-ounce jar chopped pimiento

1   cup fresh or canned mushrooms

1   to 2 cups chopped celery

4   cups (16 ounces) Cheddar cheese, grated

1   or 2 $10\frac{3}{4}$-ounce cans cream of mushroom (or cream of chicken) soup

In a 3-quart or larger saucepan boil the chicken until tender. Remove the chicken from the broth and add enough water to the chicken broth to make 2 quarts. Bring the broth and water to a boil. Add the spaghetti, season with and salt and pepper, and cook until the spaghetti is done. Drain.

In a skillet melt the margarine over medium heat and sauté the onion, green pepper, pimiento, mushrooms, and celery. Add the sautéed mixture to the spaghetti. Add the chicken, soup, and half of the cheese. Transfer to a 9 x13-inch casserole dish and top with the remaining grated cheese. Bake at 350° until the cheese is melted and the mixture is bubbly.

SERVES 4 TO 6.

Debra Talley • The Talley Trio

King Ranch Casserole

Great with refried beans and corn casserole!

1	*cup chopped onion*
1	*green bell pepper, chopped*
2	*tablespoons butter*
1	*large chicken, boiled and boned; reserve broth*
1	*10¾-ounce can cream of chicken soup*
1	*10¾-ounce can cream of mushroom soup*
1	*10-ounce can chopped tomatoes with chilies*
1	*garlic clove, minced*
1½	*tablespoons chili powder*
3	*cups (12 ounces) grated Monterey Jack cheese*
3	*cups (12 ounces) grated Cheddar cheese*
1	*package corn tortillas*

In a large saucepan melt the butter and sauté the onion and green pepper until tender. Add the remaining ingredients except the cheeses and tortillas. Let simmer and mix well.

Cut the tortillas into quarters and dip in the chicken broth to soften. Layer half of the softened tortillas in a 9 x 13-inch pan. Add half of the chicken mixture and half of the cheeses. Repeat the layers with the remaining ingredients. Bake at 350° for 45 minutes. Allow to cool for 10 minutes before serving.

SERVES 6.

Linda Reeves

Stand and Testify Mexican Chicken Casserole

1	7-ounce package Doritos
1	whole chicken, boiled and boned
1	10¾-ounce can cream of mushroom soup
1	10¾-ounce can cream of chicken soup
1	10½-ounce can chicken broth
1	onion, chopped
1	10-ounce can Ro-tel tomatoes
4	cups (1 pound) grated Longhorn cheese

Crush about half to 1 package of Doritos in the bottom of a casserole dish. Mix the chicken, soups, and the can of broth (with a little water). Pour over the Doritos. Poke holes in the casserole to let water run down to the bottom. Add the onion and tomatoes. Cover with cheese. Cover with foil and bake at 350° for 45 minutes to 1 hour.

SERVES 6.

Vicki Arnold • The Arnolds

The Arnolds of Tulsa, Oklahoma, consist of the husband-and-wife team of Frank and Vicki (center) Arnold and Tiffany Stone. Frank and Vicki host a television show, Southern Praise, *and Frank is widely respected as one of the top concert promoters in the field.*

One Way Flight Mexican Chicken

½	cup (1 stick) butter
1	large green bell pepper, diced
1	large onion, diced
1	10-ounce can Ro-tel tomatoes with green chilies
1	10¾-ounce can cream of mushroom soup
1	10¾-ounce can cream of chicken soup
1	12-ounce can evaporated milk
1	16-ounce bag Doritos chips, crushed in the bag
1	chicken, boned, and diced
1	pound Cheddar cheese, grated

In a large saucepan or skillet melt the butter and sauté the bell pepper and onion. Remove the pan from the heat and add the tomatoes, soups, and evaporated milk and mix together.

Butter a 9 x 13-inch baking dish and put half of the crushed chips on the bottom. Add the diced chicken and one-third of the cheese. Pour the soup mixture on top of the chicken, cover with the remaining cheese, and top with the remaining chips. Bake at 350° for 20 to 30 minutes or until it bubbles.

Variation: This can also be made with ground chuck substituted for the chicken.

SERVES 6.
The Telestials

Priscilla's Chicken Casserole

2	10-ounce packages frozen broccoli spears
2	cups cooked rice
4	10-ounce cans boned chicken
1	10¾-ounce can cream of chicken soup
1	8-ounce carton sour cream

Place the cooked broccoli spears along the bottom of a 9 x 13-inch casserole dish. Spread the cooked rice over the broccoli. Spread the chicken over the rice. Blend the soup and sour cream and spread over top. Bake at 350° for 20 to 25 minutes.

SERVES 6.
The McGruders

Enchanting Enchilada Casserole

1   pound ground beef

1   onion, chopped

     Salt to taste

1   10¾-ounce can cream of mushroom soup

1   10¾-ounce can cream of chicken soup

1   16-ounce can enchilada sauce

1   4-ounce can sliced black olives

12   corn tortillas, dipped in hot vegetable oil and cooled ahead of time

3   to 4 cups grated cheese

In a skillet brown the beef and onion together. Add salt sparingly. Add the soups, enchilada sauce, and olives. Simmer. In a 1½-quart baking dish layer the sauce, tortillas, and cheese alternately. Bake at 350° for 45 minutes to 1 hour.

SERVES 6.

Sonja Goff-Nolan • The Singing Goffs

The Singing Goff Family (in 1976), clockwise from bottom left, Nina, Chris, Sonja, Kevin, Randy, Cindy, and Kenny Goff, was a popular California Southern Gospel group that began as a duo in 1970 and became a family act from 1982 to 1986. They were known for the songs "It Always Gets the Darkest (Just Before Daylight)," "Walking on the Mountain Top," and "Who Is That 4th Man." Kenny and Nina now pastor a church in Mt. View, California.

Quick and Easy Chicken Enchiladas

4	chicken breasts, cooked and cut into small pieces
1	8-ounce package cream cheese (fat-free is fine)
1	teaspoon ground cumin
¼	cup frozen chopped spinach
	Salsa to taste
8	to 10 flour tortillas
1	can enchilada sauce
2	cups grated cheese (Colby Jack is suggested)

In a saucepan mix the chicken, cream cheese, cumin, spinach, and salsa. Spray a 9 x 13-inch baking dish with cooking spray. Fill the tortillas with the chicken mixture, fold, and place in the baking dish. Pour the enchilada sauce over the enchiladas. Sprinkle with cheese. Bake at 375° for 20 minutes or until the cheese is melted. Serve with sour cream.

Note: I enjoy serving this with a Catalina Mexican salad (made with lettuce, tomatoes, onion, cheese, crumbled nacho chips, 1 small can of heated Mexican or Texas-style beans, and Catalina dressing).

MAKES 8 OR 10 ENCHILADAS.

Ginger Pitchers • The Lesters

The Lesters, clockwise from top left, Brian Lester, Stephanie Mueller, Dan Pitchers, and Ginger Pitchers, are known as St. Louis's first family of gospel music.

Chilies Old Time Relleños

2	4-ounce cans green chilies, roasted and peeled
½	pound Longhorn or Monterey Jack cheese
	All-purpose flour
2	eggs, separated
⅛	teaspoon salt
¼	cup flour
	Oil for frying
	Chili sauce of choice

Remove the stem and seeds from the green chilies. Rinse carefully, so as not to tear, and drain on paper towels. Cut the cheese into the same number of strips as there are green chilies (there should be 6 to 8) and press the cheese into the chilies. Dredge the chilies in the flour. In a medium bowl whip the egg whites until stiff. In a separate bowl beat the yolks, salt, and ¼ cup of flour. Fold in the egg whites. In a skillet heat 2 inches of oil. Dip the chilies in the egg mixture and then place in the hot oil. Fry until deep brown. Turn and fry on the other side. Serve with heated chili sauce.

MAKES 6 TO 8.

The Brashear Family

Here I Am Chicken Casserole

4	large chicken breasts
1	8-ounce package cornmeal
1	8-ounce package Pepperidge Farm stuffing
½	cup (1 stick) butter or margarine, melted
1	10¾-ounce can cream of mushroom soup
1	10¾-ounce can cream of chicken soup

In a large pot of boiling warter stew the chicken (do not salt) until done. Pick the chicken off the bones. Cut the chicken into cubes and set aside. Save the broth.

In a medium bowl stir the butter into the stuffing. In a greased 1½-quart casserole dish place a layer of dressing crumbs, a layer of chicken, then a layer of mushroom soup (diluted with a broth), again a layer of crumbs, a layer of chicken, and a layer of chicken soup (diluted with a can of water). Top with the remaining crumbs and bake at 350° for 45 minutes to 1 hour or until brown. Use no salt at all.

SERVES 4.

Connie Hopper • The Hoppers

Church Choir Chicken Casserole

4	chicken breasts, cooked, boned, and cut up
1	10¾-ounce can cream of chicken soup
1	cup chopped onion (or to taste)
½	cup mayonnaise
1	15-ounce can French-style green beans, drained
1	8-ounce can sliced water chestnuts, drained
1	2-ounce jar pimientos
1	6-ounce box seasoned wild rice, cooked in chicken broth, according to package directions (Uncle Ben's original recipe wild rice is great)

In a 2-quart casserole dish combine all of the ingredients. Bake at 350° for 45 minutes or until heated through.

SERVES 4 TO 6.

Joyce Brown • The Browns

Amy's Chicken Casserole

This is my husband's favorite dish. Just after we were married, I had cooked this dish for supper one night. Being just the two of us, of course there was plenty left over. Well, the next day my husband invited his parents over for leftovers—not telling me until I had come home from the office. When I got home I discovered that the casserole had been left out all night without being refrigerated. Not wanting to poison my in-laws, I quickly prepared another casserole and no one ever knew the difference.

3	or 4 chicken breasts, cooked and cubed
1	8-ounce carton sour cream
1	10¾-ounce can cream of chicken soup
1	cup chicken broth
1	carrot, grated
½	cup (1 stick) margarine
1	8-ounce package Pepperidge Farm stuffing

In a large bowl combine the chicken, sour cream, soup, ½ cup of the broth, and the carrot. Mix well. In a saucepan melt the margarine and mix in the remaining ½ cup of broth and the stuffing. Layer the stuffing and the chicken in a casserole dish, ending with stuffiing. Bake at 325° for 30 minutes.

Note: It freezes well. (Just don't forget to put in the freezer!)

SERVES 4 TO 6.

Amy Lambert

Amy Lambert-Templeton is one of the most popular female vocalists in Southern Gospel. The solo singer has been nominated for many honors by the Singing News *Fan Awards and the* Gospel Voice *Diamond Awards. Based out of Boone, North Carolina, she has had two Top Ten singles and was featured on Bill Gaither's video* Back Home in Indiana.

HAPPY BIRTHDAYS TO YOU
Match the birthdays with the artists:

GENTLEMEN

1. Les Beasley
2. James Blackwood
3. Bill Gaither
4. Joel Hemphill
5. Jake Hess
6. Rex Nelon
7. Glen Payne
8. Brock Speer
9. J.D. Sumner
10. George Younce

A. January 19
B. February 22
C. March 28
D. August 1
E. August 4
F. August 16
G. October 20
H. November 19
I. December 24
J. December 28

Answers:
1. F, 2. E, 3. C, 4. D, 5. I, 6. A, 7. G, 8. J, 9. H, 10. B

LADIES

1. Peg McKamey Bean
2. Candy Hemphill-Christmas
3. Sheri Easter
4. Amy Lambert
5. Eva Mae LeFevre
6. Judy Martin
7. Angelina McKeithen
8. Karen Peck
9. Kelly Nelon Thompson
10. Naomi Sego

A. January 24
B. February 17
C. March 12
D. March 13
E. March 31
F. May 3
G. June 10
H. August 7
I. October 27
J. December 1

Answers:
1. E, 2. G, 3. I, 4. D, 5. H, 6. F, 7. A, 8. C, 9. J, 10. B

Chicken Spectacular

This recipe was passed down by my grandmother.

1	*6-ounce package seasoned wild rice*
2	*to 3 chicken breasts (3 cups cubed)*
1	*10¾-ounce can cream of celery soup*
1	*17-ounce can French-style green beans, drained*
1	*8-ounce can sliced water chestnuts, drained*
1	*medium onion, diced*
1	*cup mayonnaise*
	Salt and pepper to taste

Cook the rice according to the package instructions. In a large bowl mix all of the ingredients with the rice. Transfer the mixture to a greased Pyrex dish. Bake at 350° for 30 minutes.

SERVES 4.

Heather Campbell • Executive Director • SGMA Hall of Fame and Museum

Heather and John Campbell and their four-legged pal, Buster Brown.

Mrs. Luke Golden's Chicken Casserole

1	box Ritz Crackers
1	stick butter, melted
1	whole chicken, boiled, boned, and chopped
1	10¾-ounce can cream of mushroom soup
1	10¾-ounce can cream of chicken soup
½	cup sour cream
1	cup chopped water chestnuts
1	teaspoon salt
1	teaspoon pepper
1	tablespoon basil

In a medium bowl mix the crushed crackers and melted butter. Line a 9 x 13-inch casserole dish with the mixture, reserving ½ cup for the topping. Spread cooled chopped chicken over the crust. In a medium bowl mix the soups, sour cream, water chestnuts, and seasonings. Spread over the chicken and the crust. Add the remaining cracker topping. Bake at 350° until bubbly.

SERVES 6.

Brenda and William Lee Golden • The Oak Ridge Boys

Today's Oak Ridge Boys are country music superstars with Grammy, Country Music Association, and Academy of Country Music awards to go along with their Doves. The harmonious blend comes from, left to right, Joe Bonsall, William Lee Golden, Richard Sterban, and Duane Allen.

On a Journey Madras Curry

   Vegetable oil
1   onion, chopped
1   garlic clove, chopped
1   tablespoon finely chopped gingerroot
1   whole skinless chicken, boned and cut into 2- to 3-inch pieces
2   teaspoons Madras curry paste
1   tablespoon tomato paste
1   14-ounce can unsweetened coconut milk
1   teaspoon salt
1   cup water (more, if desired)
2   cubes Japanese Golden curry sauce mix
5   to 6 potatoes, peeled and cut into 2-inch pieces
   Rice, cooked

In a 4-quart pan heat the oil and brown the onion. Add the garlic and ginger and blend well. Add the chicken. Add the Madras curry paste and blend well. Add the tomato paste. Mix in the coconut milk, salt, and water. Add the Japanese Golden curry sauce mix and stir until the mix dissolves. Add more Madras curry paste, if desired. Add the potatoes. Simmer until the chicken and potatoes are cooked thoroughly. Serve over rice.

SERVES 4 TO 6.

Lori Thornton

Something Good Is About to Happen
Chicken Divan

1	bunch broccoli, parboiled
4	chicken breasts, cooked
1	10¾-ounce can 98 percent fat-free cream of chicken soup
½	cup reduced-fat mayonnaise
1	teaspoon curry powder
1	cup grated cheese
1	cup cracker crumbs (optional)

Place the broccoli in a 1-quart baking dish. Place the cut-up chicken as the next layer. In a bowl mix together the soup, mayonnaise, and curry powder; pour over the broccoli and chicken. Cover and bake at 350° for about 30 minutes. Add the cheese and cracker crumbs and bake until the cheese is melted.

SERVERS 4.

Faye Speer • The Speers

There is not a gospel group performing that has not been influenced by the music of The Speer Family. Left to right are Faye, Brock, Rosa Nell, Ben, and Mary Tom Speer.

Ernie's Grilled Chicken

½   cup ketchup

3   teaspoons brown sugar

3   tablespoons cider vinegar

1   tablespoon horseradish

1   clove garlic, minced

1   teaspoon black pepper

1   teaspoon thyme

4   skinless, boneless chicken breast halves

Preheat the grill to medium (until white ash forms on the charcoal). In a saucepan combine all of the ingredients except the chicken and bring to a boil over medium-low heat, stirring frequently for about 5 minutes until thickened.

Brush the chicken pieces with the sauce and grill sauce side down on the grill rack (or broil in a broiler pan lined with foil), about 3 inches from the heat source. Brush the top side of the chicken pieces with the sauce. Continue turning the chicken and baste with the remaining sauce for 5 to 7 minutes, until the chicken in no longer pink in the center.

SERVES 4.

Ernie Haase • The Cathedrals

Ernie Haase and wife, Lisa, who is the daughter of Cathedrals legend George Younce.

Sublime Chicken Stir Fry

4   skinless chicken breasts, boned (about 2
     pounds)

Marinade:

⅓   cup olive oil

     Juice of 3 limes

4   cloves garlic, minced

3   tablespoons fresh cilantro, chopped

½   teaspoon salt

½   teaspoon pepper

Stir-Fry:

1   tablespoon sesame oil

½   tablespoon chili oil

¼   teaspoon fresh garlic, minced

4   cups fresh broccoli

¼   chopped walnuts

1   tablespoon (low sodium) soy sauce

Visiting outside the TNN studios with longtime gospel music publicist and current Prime Time Country *producer Stacey Jo Scheirer (second from left) are Dick Clark Productions family members RAC Clark, Kari Clark, and Dick Clark.*

Pound the chicken breasts between sheets of waxed paper with a wooden mallet. Mix all of the marinade ingredients together in a medium-sized glass bowl. Put the chicken breasts in the marinade refrigerate overnight or for at least 3 hours.

Cook the chicken on a grill or broil for approximately 5 minutes per side, or until the pink is completely gone from the middle of the chicken.

In a wok on high heat, put in the sesame oil, chili oil, and garlic. Once the oil is hot, lower heat to medium and add the broccoli and walnuts. Cook for 3 to 4 minutes. Add the soy sauce and cover and cook for 1 more minute.

Serve immediately with the chicken. This dish also goes well with broiled red (and yellow and orange) peppers.

SERVES 4.

Stacey Jo Scheirer

Carson Family Honey Mustard Chicken

1	pound skinless, boneless chicken breasts
¼	cup plain yellow mustard
¼	cup liquid honey
¼	cup (½ stick) margarine, melted
	Salt and pepper to taste

To make sure that the chicken is germ free from the packer, presoak the chicken breasts in a mixture of ¼ of apple cider vinegar, ¼ cup of salt, and enough water to cover the chicken. Let soak for 30 minutes.

While the chicken is soaking, in a small bowl blend the mustard and honey together. Preheat the oven to 325°. Take the chicken out of the water, drain, and pat dry with a clean kitchen towel.

Barely melt the margarine and coat the bottom of the baking dish. Coat the chicken pieces well in the honey-mustard mixture and then place in the buttered pan. Lightly sprinkle with salt and pepper. Sprinkle more honey-mustard mixture over the top. Cover with aluminum foil and bake for 30 minutes. Check for doneness (browned on the outside and completely white on the inside.) If you would like the outside more brown, remove the foil and check every few minutes for the desired amount of brown.

This is delicious with herbed rice or Chinese vegetables.

SERVES 2 TO 3.

Martha Carson

With her "whoop-it-up" gospel style of singing, Martha Carson was known as "The Rockin' Queen of Happy Spirituals" during the 1950s when the Neon, Kentucky, native had such hits as "Rock-a My Soul," "I'm Gonna Walk and Talk With My Lord," "Let the Light Shine on Me," and "I Can't Stand Up Alone." Her philosophy to this day: "Make a joyful noise unto the Lord."

Chicken Roca

6　to 8 boneless, skinless chicken breasts

6　to 8 slices deli ham or beef

6　to 8 slices cheese (I prefer Jack)

1　10¾-ounce can cream of mushroom soup

1　8-ounce carton sour cream

Pound the chicken breasts to approximately ½-inch thickness. Place 1 slice of ham and 1 slice of cheese on each chicken breast. Roll and place in a casserole dish. Mix the soup and sour cream, and pour the mixture over the chicken. Cover and bake at 350° for 1 hour and 30 minutes to 2 hours.

SERVES 6 TO 8.

Cindy Goff • The Singing Goffs

DOWN HOME QUIZ
Match the artist or group with their hometowns:

1. Lee Roy Abernathy
2. Wendy Bagwell
3. The Blackwoods
4. Wally Fowler
5. The Goodmans
6. Jake Hess
7. Urias and Alphus LeFevre
8. Rex Nelon
9. Glen Payne
10. The Rambos
11. The Speers
12. V.O. Stamps
13. J.D. Sumner
14. James Vaughan
15. Hovie Lister
16. George Younce

A. Ackerman, Mississippi
B. Adairsville, Georgia
C. Asheville, North Carolina
D. Canton, Georgia
E. Dawson Springs, Kentucky
F. Double Springs, Georgia
G. Hiram, Georgia
H. Greenville, South Carolina
I. Jacksonville, Texas
J. Josephine, Texas
K. Lakeland, Florida
L. Lawrenceburg, Tennessee
M. Lenoir, North Carolina
N. Limestone County, Alabama
O. Sand Mountain, Alabama
P. Smithfield, Tennessee

Answers
1. D, 2. G, 3. A, 4. B, 5. O, 6. N, 7. P, 8. C, 9. J, 10. E, 11. F, 12. I, 13. K, 14. L, 15. H, 16. M

Classic Chicken and Rice Bake

5   to 6 skinless chicken breasts

     Salt, pepper, and paprika to taste

½   cup (1 stick) margarine, melted

1   tablespoon cooking sherry

4   cups water

1   cup regular rice

½   teaspoon salt

½   teaspoon dried basil

1   teaspoon dried rosemary

1   teaspoon dried marjoram

4   chicken bouillon cubes

½   cup (1 stick) margarine

1   cup sour cream

½   cup mayonnaise

1   teaspoon paprika

1   tablespoon parsley

Sprinkle the chicken with salt, pepper, and paprika. Place in a 1½-quart casserole dish and pour the melted butter over the chicken. Sprinkle cooking sherry over each piece. Cover and bake at 350° for 1 hour. Bone the chicken.

In a covered pot combine the water, rice, salt, basil, rosemary, marjoram, bouillon, and ½ cup of margarine and boil for 20 minutes.

Remove the chicken from the pan and add the sour cream, mayonnaise, paprika, and parsley to the pan drippings to make a sauce. Assemble the ingredients into 2 baking dishes. Alternate rice, half of the sauce, chicken, and then the remaining sauce. Cover and bake at 350° for 45 minutes to 1 hour.

SERVES 4 TO 6.

Nina Goff • The Singing Goffs

Albert's "Hand Warmin' Chicken" Country Style

1	3-pound chicken
½	cup all-purpose flour
2	teaspoons salt
6	tablespoons butter
6	medium potatoes
6	small onions
6	large carrots
2	large green bell peppers
1	tablespoon sugar
¼	teaspoon black pepper
2½	cups stewed tomatoes
3	cups boiling water

Albert E. Brumley was one of Southern Gospel's greatest songwriters, having more than five hundred of his songs recorded. Born in Indian Territory, Brumley studied at the old Hartford Institute at Hartford, Arkansas, and began writing tunes for the Hartford Music Company, which he later owned. Among his credits are "I'll Fly Away," "Jesus Hold My Hand," "Turn Your Radio On," and "I'll Meet You in the Morning." An annual Albert E. Brumley Sun-Up to Sundown Sing is held each August in Springdale, Arkansas.

Dress the chicken and wipe with a damp cloth. Mix ½ teaspoon of the salt with the flour and roll the chicken in the mixture. Melt the butter in a frying pan and brown the chicken on all sides over high heat for about 10 minutes.

Peel the skins from the potatoes and the onions. Scrape and quarter the carrots lengthwise. Seed the green peppers and slice them in ½-inch strips. Mix the remaining salt with the sugar, black pepper, and tomatoes. Place ⅔ of the vegetables in the bottom of a heavy kettle. Place the chicken on top and add the remaining vegetables. Pour the tomato mixture and the boiling water over all. Cover tightly and bring to a boil. Reduce heat and let simmer until tender, about 1 hour and 30 minutes.

SERVES 6.

Albert E. Brumley

Granny's Favorite Lemon Fried Chicken

This is the favorite dish of Granny (Jack's mother, Carrie Toney). Whenever she feels bad and doesn't have much appetite, she wants this fried chicken.

1   *fryer, skinned and washed (or just the breasts or your favorite parts)*

      Lemon-pepper seasoning

      Salt

      All-purpose flour

      Canola oil

Sprinkle each piece of chicken individually with lemon-pepper seasoning and salt. Dredge the chicken in flour to coat. In a skillet heat an adequate amount of canola oil for frying and cook over medium to high heat until the chicken is as brown as you desire. Drain on paper towels.

Gail and Jack Toney • The Statesmen

GOSPEL TV TIME
Match to the group the show they hosted or appeared on:

1. The Arnolds
2. The Florida Boys
3. The Happy Goodman Family
4. The Hemphills
5. The LeFevres
6. The Ranger Trio and The Chuck Wagon Gang
7. The Statesmen Quartet

A. *Family Time*
B. *Gospel Roundup*
C. *Gospel Singing Caravan*
D. *Gospel Singing Jubilee and The Gospel Songshop*
E. *Gospel Singing Jubilee*
F. *Singin' Time in Dixie*
G. *Southern Praise*

Answers
1. G, 2. D, 3. E, 4. A, 5. C, 6. B, 7. F

Jake's Oven-Fried Chicken Parmesan

1	cup crushed herb stuffing (Pepperidge Farm)
2/3	cup grated Parmesan cheese
1/4	cup chopped fresh parsley
1	garlic clove, minced (optional)
1/2	cup (1 stick) butter, melted
2 1/2	to 3 pounds boneless chicken breasts

In a shallow bowl combine the stuffing crumbs, Parmesan cheese, parsley, and garlic. Dip the chicken pieces in the butter and roll in the crumbs. Place the pieces in a shallow pan skin side up and not touching. Sprinkle with the remaining butter and crumbs. Bake at 350° for 45 minutes, or until tender. Do not turn.

SERVES 8.

Jake Hess

Jake Hess is one of the most dominant personalities in the field of gospel music. In 1948, he began his longtime relationship with Hovie Lister and The Statesmen Quartet. In 1963 he organized The Imperials. Today he performs solo as a part of The Bill Gaither Homecoming concerts.

Up Yonder Rolled Chicken Breasts

1   4.5 ounce can chopped beef

4   boneless chicken breasts

8   strips bacon

1   cup sour cream

1   10¾-ounce can cream of mushroom soup

Line a 1-quart casserole dish with the beef. Roll the chicken breasts up with bacon, secure with toothpicks and place on the beef. Mix together the sour cream and soup and pour over the chicken. Bake at 300° for 1 hour and 30 minutes.

   Note: My family likes for me to substitute Hidden Valley ranch dressing for the sour cream.

SERVES 4.

Polly Lewis Copsey • The Lewis Family

Left to right in this 1970s Lewis Family photograph are Polly, Miggie, and Janis.

Speak to the Mountain Chicken Breasts

This is Jeff's favorite.

4   ounces dried beef

4   to 6 boneless chicken breasts

1   cup sour cream

1   10¾-ounce can cream of mushroom soup

Line a buttered baking dish with the beef. Place the chicken on top of the beef. Spread a layer of sour cream over the beef. Spread the soup over the sour cream. Bake uncovered at 300° for 1 hour and 30 minutes.

SERVES 4 TO 6.

Jeff and Sheri Easter

Jeff and Sheri Easter share smiles for their first album cover in 1987.

Polly's Lemon Pepper Trio

I love to cook, and one of my favorite seasonings is lemon pepper. Here are three "quick" recipes with this seasoning.

Lemon Pepper Chicken

Place chicken breasts in the bottom of a casserole dish. (Use as many breasts as you prefer to cook.) Sprinkle lemon pepper generously and a little salt on each piece. Cover and bake at 400° oven for about 25 minutes. Remove the dish from the oven and turn each breast over and sprinkle the new top side with more lemon pepper and a little salt. (Hint: Go easy on the lemon pepper until you determine how much you like.) Bake an additional 20 minutes or until done.

Note: Don't add water and always skin the chicken. This is a low-fat dish. It only has chicken and seasonings.

Lemon Pepper Salmon

Open a can of salmon and break large pieces of fish into a small casserole dish. Sprinkle with lemon pepper. Bake at 400° for about 10 minutes.

Lemon Pepper Asparagus

Open a can of asparagus tips. Pour into a microwavable dish. Sprinkle generously with lemon pepper seasoning and dot with butter. Microwave until the butter is melted. Serve hot.

Polly Lewis Copsey • The Lewis Family

The Lewis Family in the 1960s were, left to right, Little Roy, Miggie, Pop, Polly, Wallace, Janis, and Lewis Phillips.

Kathy's Leftover Turkey Surprise

Although I seldom have leftovers of any kind!

1	*5.25-ounce package au gratin potatoes*
2	*cups cubed cooked turkey*
2	*cups mixed frozen vegetables, thawed and drained*
1/2	*teaspoon dried thyme leaves*
1/4	*cup grated Cheddar cheese*

In a 2-quart casserole prepare the potatoes as directed on the package. Stir in the turkey, vegetables, and thyme, and mix well. Bake at 400° for 40 to 45 minutes. Sprinkle with Cheddar cheese. Bake for an additional 1 to 2 minutes. Let stand for 5 minutes.

SERVES 4.

Kathy Williams • Homeland Records

Typical Day Pork Chops and Rice

4	*to 6 pork chops*
1	*cup rice, uncooked*
2	*10 1/2-ounce cans beef consommé*
1	*onion, sliced*
1	*tomato, sliced*
1	*green bell pepper, sliced*
	Salt and pepper to taste

In a skillet brown the pork chops. In a 9 x 13-inch pan mix the rice and consommé. Place the pork chops on the rice mixture. Place 1 slice of onion, 1 slice of tomato, and one ring of bell pepper on each pork chop. Add salt and pepper. Bake at 350° for 1 or hour or until the juice is absorbed.

SERVES 4 TO 6.

Lori Thornton

Songbook Sweet and Sour Pork

3	tablespoons oil
2½	pounds lean pork shoulder, cut into cubes
8	slices onion
1½	cups pineapple juice
½	cup water
½	cup vinegar
½	cup firmly packed brown sugar
1½	teaspoon salt
1	cup diced green bell pepper
2	20-ounce cans pineapple chunks
2	tablespoons soy sauce
5	tablespoons cornstarch
½	cup water

In a large skillet heat the oil and brown the pork cubes and onion slices. Add the pineapple juice, water, vinegar, brown sugar, and salt. Cover and cook until tender. Reduce the heat and add the green pepper, pineapple chunks, and soy sauce. In a small bowl mix the cornstarch and water and add to the skillet mixture. Cook until thickened, stirring constantly. Serve over rice.

SERVES 8.

Gussie Mae Goodman Rogers • The Happy Goodmans

Hymn Ham Casserole

My family likes this dish. It's almost a meal by itself.

¼   cup (½ stick) butter
½   cup all-purpose flour
4   cups milk
1   cup whipping cream
      Salt and pepper to taste
2   pounds cooked ham, cut into small pieces
2   pounds Irish potatoes, diced and cooked
1   10-ounce package frozen English peas

In a large saucepan melt the butter. Add the flour and stir in until smooth. Add the milk and whipping cream. Cook over medium heat , stirring constantly, until smooth and thickened. Season to taste. In a large casserole dish combine the ham, cooked potatoes, and frozen peas. Pour the milk mixture over the top and stir lightly. Bake at 375° for 40 to 50 minutes or until browned and bubbly on top.

SERVES 6 TO 8.

Naomi Sego Reader • Naomi and the Segos

The Sego Brothers & Naomi were one of the most popular family groups of the 1960s. Pictured here, left to right, are James, Naomi, Lamar, and W.R. Sego, and two unidentified musicians.

That's Using the Ol' Noodle!

We were having dinner with about 30 other singers and promoters at one of Hollywood's most famous Italian restaurants. The waitress was serving our table when she made an abrupt turn between my husband and the person next to him. One of the plates with spaghetti and meatballs struck him just above the ear. All of the food on the plate slipped over the top of his head, and he sat there with spaghetti hanging down, three meatballs on top of his head, and lots of juice dripping. He counted from ten to one, then started to laugh with all the others. The waitress fainted.

Naomi Sego Reader

"Unwanted Guest" Ham

During Christmas holidays one year, our family decided to bake a ham. We bought a pre-cooked ham, took the wrapping off, and started fixing it. We sliced several slits on top of the ham, filled each slit with pineapple. We put cloves on the bottom and sides. We added glaze several times while it was baking. We glazed it over and over again, smelling the delicious aroma. This was going to be our Christmas Eve supper. When we served the ham, we started to slice it and discovered that we had left the plastic on it! So...if you ever have an "unwanted guest," serve them this ham. For your own ham, take off the plastic.

1	*pre-cooked ham*
	Cloves
1	*16-ounce can sliced pineapple, reserving juice*
8	*ounces brown sugar*

Stick cloves into the bottom and sides of the ham. Cut several slits on top of the ham. Fill some of the slits with some of the pineapple slices. Add the brown sugar to the pineapple juice and pour a little of the mixture over the ham. Take 3 of the pineapple slices and place on top of the ham while cooking. Bake at 300° for 2 or 3 hours. Pour the remaining brown sugar mixture over the ham during baking.

SERVES A FAMILY.

The Telestials

Restaurant-Style Smoked Ribs

We always celebrate my wife's birthday by going to a restaurant of her choice. One year Debbie chose Tony Roma's, a restaurant well known for its delicious ribs.

After we had been seated and ordered our meal, I excused myself under the pretense of finding the restroom. Instead, I went around to where the hostess was and ordered a dessert with birthday candles and asked that the waiters and waitresses gather around Debbie and sing "Happy Birthday" (as they often do at restaurants). The hostess assured me that she would let our waitress know and told me to "nod" at our waitress when I was ready for them to sing.

I returned to our table rather proud of myself and looking forward to Debbie's being surprised and a little embarrassed by the unexpected attention.

We enjoyed a great meal and when the waitress came around to check on us, I gave her a little nod and smile. She looked at me as if to say, "What's wrong with you?"

Debbie didn't have a clue at this point and we waited for quite a while. I finally caught the eye of the waitress again. This time I nodded and gave her a little wink and a smile to let her know that we were ready for the surprise. She gave me a weak smile back, and by now she was, I'm sure, thinking, "This man is the biggest flirt I have ever seen — and right in front of his wife!"

After three or four attempts to get the message to her, she just brought us our check. I finally had to come out and say to her, "I'm ready now." The waitress replied, "Ready for what?" I said, "Did you not get the message?" The waitress answered, "The message about what?"

Need I say more? The hostess had been busy and forgot to tell our waitress what was supposed to be happening. The joke was on me. I was the one who was surprised and a little embarrassed — much to Debbie's delight!

When I'm not game for ribbing at a restaurant, here is my recipe for delicious smoked ribs that you can cook at home. You can buy a smoker for around thirty dollars at stores such as Wal-Mart, K-Mart, Target, etc.

We usually smoke country-style pork ribs, and it makes all the difference in the world if you take the time to marinate them overnight in Worcestershire sauce (we use Lea & Perrins) before cooking them. This tenderizes the meat and adds greatly to the taste!

You should soak your hickory (wood) chunks, completely submerged in water for 30 minutes before starting the smoking process. Also spray the racks and inside of the dome top of the smoker with a non-stick cooking spray. You will be placing the ribs on either the top or bottom (or both) cooking racks in the smoker. Fill the water pan just below the bottom rack ¾ full of water.

The charcoal pan is at the very bottom of the smoker. Arrange the charcoal to where it forms a pyramid in the center about 2 inches above the rim of the charcoal pan. If you are using charcoal that requires the use of lighter fluid, cover the briquettes liberally and allow the lighter fluid to soak in for about a minute before igniting. The briquettes will flame up for about 15 minutes. As soon as the flame begins to die out, spread the charcoal briquettes evenly in the charcoal pan and place 3 to 6 hickory chunks on top of the smoldering charcoal.

Now you are ready to place the ribs on the rack(s) and cover the smoker. It takes about 3 to 4 hours for the ribs to cook using this method. (I usually start about 9 a.m. and the ribs are ready to eat at 12:30.)

You still want to baste the ribs 3 to 4 times while they are cooking. I recommend the following secret concoction:

½   *cup your favorite barbecue sauce*

¼   *cup steak sauce*

3   *tablespoons honey*

Mix all of these together in one container and use a brush to baste the ribs after about an hour. Baste the meat again after the second and third hours and one last time just before taking the ribs out of the smoker. (The smoker needs to stay covered as much as possible, so resist the urge to peek except when you are basting the meat.)

Follow these directions and you will have a delicious meal that you can cook anywhere, anytime of the year.

Debbie and Rick Francis

Familiar faces in Southern Gospel, Rick Francis and wife Debbie share grins for a Christmas pose.

Call Your Friends Sauerkraut and Sausage

As our family members got older, got married, and started having families of their own, it became increasingly more difficult for everyone to come to Mom and Dad's house for Christmas. Since we are a close family and always liked to celebrate holidays together, we needed a solution.

So, in 1992, Dad, whom many people knew as "Pops," started a tradition in our family of having a Christmas Eve party with all the family members. The twist for his party was that only the men could cook. It was Dad's favorite day of the year, and he would cook up a storm. His favorite thing to make was one of Mom's German recipes for sauerkraut and sausage, and we looked forward to eating it. Even though Dad passed away in 1996, we still carry on the tradition of our Christmas Eve celebration and enjoy good fun, good fellowship, and good sauerkraut and sausage.

2   *16- to 20-ounce bags sauerkraut*

3   *tablespoons applesauce*

1   *pound kielbasa sausage*

1   *pound sweet sausage*

1   *pound hot sausage*

Place the sauerkraut in a crockpot and mix in the applesauce (the applesauce tames the taste of the sauerkraut). Then slice the sausage into bite-sized pieces and put the pieces into the crockpot. Let it simmer anywhere from 8 to 20 hours until the sausage is tender and juicy. (The longer it cooks, the better it is!) It's good to serve over or with mashed potatoes.

SERVES 10.

The Merediths

The Merediths, left to right, Larry Shaw, Alesia Meredith, and Brett Meredith, of Swansea, South Carolina, have recorded five albums since 1992. The group was formed in 1984 as a hobby for the family but by 1990 their harmonizing for fun became a career. Alesia penned their Top Twenty hit "Roses Blooming." The Merediths have visited more than two hundred Salvation Army organizations.

Front Porch Barbecue Glaze

Growing up with my family, we spent many hours together on the front porch. Now that I've grown and have a family of my own, we seem to gravitate to the deck in the back yard. That's where the grill is! Here is one of our favorite glazes for ribs or chicken prepared on the grill. Give it a try and discover neighbors you never you knew you had!

1   *cup apricot preserves*

2   *tablespoons lime juice*

1   *tablespoon soy sauce*

½   *teaspoon grated gingerroot (or ¼ teaspoon ground ginger)*

⅛   *teaspoon ground red pepper*

In a 1-quart saucepan combine all of the ingredients, heat, and stir till it bubbles. It's ready now or you can cover it and chill it for up to 5 days.

MAKES ABOUT 1 CUP.

Mark Bishop • The Bishops

Mark Bishop (right) joins Jerry Goff in applause during a Southern Gospel concert at Nashville's Ryman Auditorium.

Going Back Salmon Patties

1	15½-ounce can salmon
3	tablespoons butter or margarine, melted
½	cup all-purpose flour
1½	cups milk
1	egg
¼	teaspoon salt
⅛	teaspoon pepper
⅓	cup finely chopped onion
1½	teaspoons baking powder
¼	cup all-purpose flour
1½	cups vegetable oil

Drain the salmon, reserving 2 tablespoons of salmon liquid. Flake the salmon. In a saucepan melt the butter and blend in the ½ cup of flour. Slowly add the milk and stir constantly until thick. Add the egg, salt, and pepper and mix well. Stir in the salmon and onion. In a small bowl blend the baking powder and 2 tablespoons of salmon liquid, and then add to the mixture. Shape into 4 patties and roll them lightly in the ¼ cup of flour. In a skillet or deep pan heat the oil to about 375° and fry the salmon patties in the hot oil. Drain on paper towels.

SERVES 4.

The Freemans

The Freemans formed as a family ministry more than twenty years ago when Darrell Freeman began playing bass guitar with his family in The Pathways in Sandusky, Ohio. His wife Chris was a member of The Hinsons and twice named queen of gospel music by the readers of The Singing News in the mid-1970s. Today The Freemans are, left to right, drummer Nick Hodges, Joe Freeman, Chris Freeman, Misty Freeman (Chris and Darrell's daughter), and Darrell Freeman.

❧ SIDE DISHES ❧

Grandpa Beans

2	pounds brown beans, cooked and drained
1	pound hamburger, browned (seasoned with salt and pepper)
½	cup ketchup
1	cup firmly packed brown sugar
¾	cup chili powder
¼	cup vinegar
1	8-ounce can tomato sauce or paste
1	teaspoon salt
1	teaspoon pepper
1	teaspoon celery salt
1	teaspoon onion salt
1	teaspoon Worcestershire sauce
1	teaspoon seasoned salt

In a large pot combine the cooked beans and hamburger. Add the remaining ingredients and mix well. Simmer to heat through, stirring occasionally.

SERVES 6 TO 8.

Dale Halyard • The Singing Halyards

Sherry's All-American Baked Beans

During the Fourth of July, we enjoy a time of being with family for cookouts, fireworks, and fun. This is one of our family's favorite foods during this time of year.

3	16-ounce cans pork and beans
½	cup Bull's Eye with honey barbecue sauce
1	pound ground beef
1	onion, chopped
1	bell pepper, chopped
	Cajun seasoning to taste
3	slices bacon

In a 2½-quart round casserole dish combine the beans and barbecue sauce. In a skillet brown the hamburger meat and drain off the excess fat. Add the onion, bell pepper, and Cajun seasoning to the skillet and cook until browned. Pour the skillet mixture into the beans mixture. Place bacon strips on top and bake uncovered in a 375° oven for 35 to 44 minutes.

SERVES 8 TO 10.

Sherry and Jeff Steele • The Steeles

The Steeles in this 1984 performance included (left to right) Faith Hill, Jeff Steele, and Sherry Steele.

The Steeles of Gallatin, Tennessee, had their tune "I Must Tell Somebody" named song of the year by The Gospel Voice *magazine in 1994. Among their Number One hits are "God Kept His Promise" and "We Want America Back." Country music star Faith Hill is an alumnus of the group. Pictured here are Sherry and Jeff Steele.*

Amen Green Beans Amandine

1   **pound frozen or canned French-style green beans**

     Salt to taste (optional)

2   **tablespoons slivered almonds**

2   **tablespoons butter or margarine**

1   **teaspoon lemon juice**

In a saucepan cook the green beans with a little bit of water. Season with salt, if desired. Drain and transfer to a serving dish.

   In a skillet or small saucepan over low heat, cook the almonds in the butter or margarine, stirring occasionally, until golden. Remove from the heat and pour over the green beans.

SERVES 4.

Ken Fuquay • Jericho

Jericho was founded in 1993 by Dwayne Burke, a longtime member of The Singing Americans. They were nominated as Horizon Group of the Year in the 1994 Gospel Voice Diamond Awards. Left to right are Kelly Paris, Dwayne Burke, Milan Klipa, and Ken Fuquay.

Bring It on Home Broccoli Casserole

2	eggs, well beaten
1	cup mayonnaise
1	10¾-ounce can cream of mushroom soup
1	cup sharp Cheddar cheese, grated
1	medium onion, chopped
2	10-ounce packages frozen chopped broccoli, cooked and drained
	Crushed Ritz crackers

Preheat the oven to 350°. In a large mixing bowl mix together the eggs, mayonnaise, soup, cheese, and onion. Stir in the drained broccoli. Pour the mixture into a greased 9-inch round baking dish and bake for 30 minutes. Top with crushed Ritz crackers and bake for 15 minutes more.

SERVES 6.

Miggie and Mom Lewis • The Lewis Family

Mom and Pop Lewis celebrating their 50th wedding anniversary in 1965.

Mom Lewis at the record table in the 1960s.

Lewis Family Glazed Carrots

2   **tablespoons butter**

2   **teaspoons grated onion**

2   **tablespoons light brown sugar**

1   **2-pound package carrots, boiled, drained, and sliced (or 2 16-ounce cans sliced carrots, drained)**

In a heavy skillet melt the butter. Add the onion and cook for 1 to 2 minutes until tender. Add the brown sugar and stir until dissolved. Slowly toss the carrots in the glaze until shiny. Serve hot.

   Note: I prefer to cut my carrots into long, slender pieces.

SERVES 6 TO 8.

Polly Lewis Copsey • The Lewis Family

Gathering at the river in this 1960s photograph are Lewis Family members, left to right, Miggie, Janis, and Polly.

Kelly's Marinated Carrots

2   pounds carrots, sliced

1   green bell pepper, sliced into rings

1   medium onion, thinly sliced

1   10¾-ounce can tomato soup

     Salt and pepper to taste

½   cup salad oil

1   cup sugar

¾   cup vinegar

1   teaspoon prepared mustard

1   teaspoon Worcestershire sauce

In a large pot boil the carrots in salty water until fork tender. Cool the carrots.

   In a 2-quart casserole dish alternate layers of carrots, pepper rings, and onion slices. In a medium bowl combine the remaining ingredients and beat until well blended. Pour the mixture over the vegetables and refrigerate overnight.

SERVES 4 TO 6.

Kelly Paris • Jericho

Sunshine Carrots

7   or 8 medium carrots

1   tablespoon sugar

1   teaspoon cornstarch

¼   teaspoon ground ginger

¼   teaspoon salt

¼   cup orange juice

2   tablespoons butter

   Parsley

   Orange twists

Slice the carrots crosswise into ½-inch thick slices. In a medium pot cook the carrots in boiling salted water for 10 to 15 minutes or until tender. Drain and transfer to a serving dish.

In a small saucepan combine the sugar, cornstarch, ginger, and salt. Add the orange juice and cook, stirring constantly until thickened and bubbly. Boil for 1 minute and remove from heat. Stir in the butter. Pour over the hot carrots and toss to coat evenly. Garnish with parsley and an orange twist.

SERVES 4.

Jo (Mrs. Herman) Harper • Harper & Associates

A dream comes true—According to Jo Harper, this is the first official photograph of Harper & Associates.

Gold City Baked Apples

1	apple for each person
3	tablespoons raisins per apple
2	tablespoons chopped pecans per apple
¼	cup apple juice per apple
	Ground cinnamon
1	marshmallow per apple

Peel the apples halfway down and core. Stuff the core with the raisins and nuts. Place the apples in a baking pan and pour the juice over the apples. Sprinkle cinnamon over each apple. Bake at 375° for 40 to 45 minutes.

Top each apple with a marshmallow for the last 2 to 5 minutes, until melted.

Doug Riley • Gold City Quartet

Friendly Folks Fried Okra

24	tender pods okra
	Salt and pepper to taste
	All-purpose flour
	Cornmeal
	Oil

Clean and wash the okra. Cut off each end and then cut into ¼-inch portions. Place the okra into a large bowl and sprinkle with salt, pepper, flour, and cornmeal, using equal parts flour and cornmeal. Stir or toss until the pieces are completely coated. Cover the bottom of an electric frying pan with oil and place over medium heat. Add the okra, cover with a lid, and fry, stirring frequently until brown and tender. Serve hot.

SERVES 4.

Mr. and Mrs. Les Beasley

Coming Home Cabbage and Apple Casserole

1   *small head red cabbage*

1   *small head green cabbage*

     Salt and pepper to taste

½   *cup butter*

½   *cup firmly packed brown sugar*

     Juice of 1 lemon

¼   *teaspoon grated nutmeg*

3   *cups diced apples*

1   *cup minced green bell pepper*

     Buttered breadcrumbs

Grind the red and green cabbage separately. Season the red cabbage with salt and pepper and place in a greased 9 x 13-inch or 3-quart casserole dish. Dot with butter. In a small bowl combine the the sugar, lemon juice, and nutmeg, and sprinkle over the apples. Layer the apples on top of the red cabbage. Mix the green cabbage with the green pepper, season with salt and pepper, and place over the apples. Dot with butter. Cover with the buttered breadcrumbs. Bake at 350° for about 25 minutes

SERVES 8.

Randall Franks • The Marksmen

The Marksmen are a popular bluegrass gospel group out of Murrayville, Georgia, that was formed by Earle Wheeler and dates back to 1967. Earle's son Mark Wheeler is lead singer and a top gospel songwriter. Pictured in this 1988 photograph are Earle Wheeler, front, and, left to right, Mark Wheeler, Darrin Chambers, Randall Franks, Rob Gillentine, and Keith Chambers.

Sumner Squash Casserole

3   cups cooked yellow zucchini

6   tablespoons (¾ stick) margarine

2   eggs

1   teaspoon salt

½   teaspoon pepper

1   or 2 onions, chopped

1   cup grated Colby cheese

2   cups cracker crumbs

In a large bowl stir all the ingredients together. Transfer the mixture to a 2-quart casserole dish. Bake at 350° for 40 minutes.

SERVES 6.

J. D. Sumner

The Stamps, circa 1965, featured, clockwise from bottom right, Jimmy Blackwood, J.D. Sumner, Jim Hill, Jim "Duke" Dumas, Tony Brown, Donnie Sumner (J.D.'s cousin), and Mylon LeFevre.

J.D. Sumner and The Stamps

J.D. Sumner and The Stamps

J.D. Sumner and the Stamps Quartet

J.D. Sumner & The Stamps Quartet are to Southern Gospel what Babe Ruth was to baseball. They can hit (all the notes), pitch (their voices perfectly), and steal (the show).

Sumner is recognized by *The Guinness Book of World Records* as the world's lowest bass singer, and at six-foot-six-inches tall he may also be Southern Gospel's tallest bass singer.

"The only way I can describe my voice is saying I've been blessed by God," says Sumner.

The bass great has been leading the Stamps for nearly thirty years, and among the highlights of their career are the many regular performances with Elvis Presley at a time when his star was shining brightest. Of course, Sumner also made a mark as bass singer with The Blackwood Brothers, joining that group in 1954 after the tragic plane crash that took the lives of R.W. Blackwood and Bill Lyles.

During the 1940s Sumner had performed with such quartets as The Stamps Sunny South Quartet and the Dixie Lily Harmoneers. In 1949, he moved on to The Sunshine Boys, but it was his stint with The Blackwood Brothers that gave Sumner his chance to stamp his indelible brand on Southern Gospel with his innovative notions.

Sumner, a noted songwriter with more than five hundred songs to his credit, is a creative force who has loaned his talents to the betterment of the gospel music industry in more ways than one. He helped found the Gospel Music Association and was responsible for the development of national gospel music publications. His brainchild resulted in a monthly newsletter, *Good News,* published by the Gospel Music Association, which has since grown into *The Singing News,* "the printed voice of gospel music." And it was Sumner who came up with the idea of The National Quartet Convention.

With a history dating back to 1924, the Stamps lay claim to being the longest performing male quartet in the business. Sumner, who spent

J.D. Sumner and The Stamps boast one of the longest-running male quartets in gospel history, originating in 1924. The Stamps Quartet performed regularly with Elvis Presley during the height of his career. Surrounding J.D. Sumner, left to right, are Jerry Kelso, Ed Enoch, Ed Hill, and Rick Strickland.

most the 1950s with The Blackwood Brothers, began reworking The Stamps Quartet in the mid-1960s after he and James and Cecil Blackwood acquired The Stamps Quartet and the Stamps Quartet Music Company from Frank Stamps in 1963.

It was about this time that Sumner and Blackwood reorganized the Stamps Quartet with Jerry Redd as tenor, Terry Blackwood singing lead, Roger McDuff singing baritone, and Big John Hall as bass. Smilin' Joe Roper served as pianist and manager. In 1965, Sumner swapped places with Hall to become bass singer with The Stamps Quartet, while Hall joined the Blackwoods. From that time forward, J.D. Sumner and The Stamps have maintained a major force in the arena of gospel music. Members through the years have included, Jim Hill, Mylon Lefevre, Tony Brown, Donnie Sumner, Richard Sterban, Jimmy and Billy Blackwood, Bill Baize, Dave Rowland and today's Stamps Quartet of Sumner, lead singer Ed Enoch, baritone Ed Hill, and tenor Rick Strickland. Jerry Kelso adds support as keyboard technician.

It was their overall quality, uniqueness, and expertise that won The Stamps a coveted spot in the Elvis Presley's concerts, films, and recordings from 1971 through the last six years of the entertainer's life.

The Stamps are the only major Southern gospel group whose repertoire includes secular standards and country & western tunes along with the gospel sounds.

The Stamps Baxter School of Music continues to convene annually in Nashville.

Lead singer and road manager Enoch has been one of the Stamps since 1969. It was Presley himself who often introduced Enoch during Elvis' road shows with the words "... the greatest voice to ever come out of gospel music."

Baritone Hill has sung with the quartet since 1974, and possesses the booming voice that once rang across concert halls with the immortal line "Ladies and gentlemen, Elvis has left the building. Goodbye, and God bless you."

The history of The Stamps is closely connected with the history of Southern gospel and dates back to the early 1920s. The name Stamps itself has been a household word when people think of gospel music—especially in connection with singing conventions, singing schools, and gospel songbooks.

The Stamps Quartet traces its roots to a farmer and sawmill man, William Oscar Stamps, who settled with his family near Gilmer in Upshur County, Texas. The community near the sawmill took on the name of Stamps since most of the folks worked in the sawmill or were farmers.

The citizens decided to build and school and church building, and W.O. Stamps donated the land and lumber. Soon the area had a school for the children on weekdays and a church on Sundays, which was used by various denominations, primarily Methodist.

W.O. and Florence Stamps had six sons: Charlie, Oscar, Hampton, Virgil, Frank, and Fred. All of them are believed to have been gospel singers, but Frank and Virgil (V.O.) were the most renowned. It was V.O. who opened an office in Jacksonville, Texas, where he began compiling and editing a songbook called *Harbor Bells,* and Frank hit the road performing with a quartet to advertise the new music company. That original Stamps Quartet in 1924 included Frank Stamps, J.E. Wheeler, Lee Myers, and J.E. Hamilton.

By 1926 that first quartet had disbanded, and V.O. sold forty-nine percent of the business to J.R. Baxter Jr. of Chattanooga, Tennessee, to form the Stamps-Baxter Music Company in Dallas.

Thus, in 1927, a new Stamps Quartet was put together behind the strong piano playing of Dwight Brock. Frank Stamps sang bass, while Palmer Wheeler was first tenor, Roy Wheeler sang second tenor, and Odis Echols handled baritone. This All-Star Quartet became a most entertaining fivesome.

Frank signed a contract with the Victor Talking Machine Company, and on October 20, 1927, in Atlanta, they became the first gospel quartet to record for a major record label. The first two songs recorded for disc were "Give the World a Smile" and "Love Leads the Way." The record sold just shy of one million copies.

Then, in 1936 at the Texas Centennial, V.O. Stamps made a deal with Dallas radio station KRLD to broadcast the group. The group's program immediately became the most popular show on the station. During their air time, the Stamps offered a songbook for one dollar, and in the first month more than thirty thousand offers came through the mail. Business was booming as was the sound of The Stamps.

Now, nearly some sixty years later, The Stamps Quartet, under the guiding eye of J.D. Sumner, continues as one of the most visible and well-respected names in the history of Southern Gospel.

Boarding a plane in this vintage picture are The Stamps' members, left to right, Jimmy Blackwood, Chuck Ramsey, Jim Hill, Roger McDuff, and J.D. Sumner.

SOUL MATES
Match the singing couples by their first names:

1.	Bo	A.	Chris
2.	Brock	B.	Connie
3.	Claude	C.	Debra
4.	Darrell	D.	Dixie
5.	Howard	E.	Faye
6.	Jeff	F.	Kelly
7.	Jerry	G.	LaBreeska
8.	Joel	H.	Peg
9.	Kevin	I.	Rhoda
10.	Roger	J.	Sheri
11.	Ruben	K.	Tammy
12.	Tim	L.	Vestal

Answers
1. I (Hinson); 2. E (Speer); 3. B (Hopper); 4. A (Freeman); 5. L (Goodman); 6. J (Easter); 7. F (Thompson); 8. G (Hemphill); 9. K (Spencer); 10. C (Talley); 11. H (Bean); 12. D (McKeithen)

The Yodeler's Casserole

1	10-ounce package frozen carrots
1	10-ounce package frozen broccoli
1	10-ounce package frozen cauliflower
1	10-ounce package frozen Brussels sprouts
1	10¾-ounce can cream of mushroom soup
1	5-ounce jar Cheez-Whiz
1	2.8-ounce can French-fried onion rings

Cook all of the vegetables for half the time stated in the package directions. Transfer the vegetables to a 2½-ounce casserole dish. In a saucepan heat and blend the condensed soup and cheese. Pour over the vegetables and carefully mix. Bake at 375° for 30 minutes. Top with the onion rings during the last 5 minutes.

Variation: Frozen onions can be used in the casserole. If you use them, omit the French-fried onion rings.

SERVES 8 TO 10.

Margo Smith

Halyards Hominy Casserole

2	15½-ounce cans yellow hominy, drained
2	jalapeño peppers, diced
1	medium onion, chopped and sautéed
1	8-ounce carton sour cream
1	teaspoon chili powder
	Dash salt
½	pound Cheddar cheese, grated

In a 2-quart casserole dish combine the hominy, jalapeños, onion, sour cream, chili powder, and salt. Add a little of the cheese to the mixture. Mix well. Bake at 350° for 30 minutes.

Add the remainder of the cheese as topping just before removing from the oven.

SERVES 6.

Sadie Halyard • The Singing Halyards

Crown the King Corn Pudding Casserole

½   cup (1 stick) margarine, softened

1   cup sour cream

1   8½-ounce box Jiffy corn muffin mix

1   egg

1   15-ounce can whole kernel corn, drained

1   15-ounce can cream style corn

     Pinch of salt

In a large bowl mix all of the ingredients together. Pour into a greased 2-quart casserole or 9-inch square pan. Bake at 375° for 1 hour.

SERVES 6 TO 8.

Linda Reeves

Linda Reeves is a singer, songwriter, speaker, and dedicated member of the Indiana Gospel Music Association.

He's Still Working on Me Corn Casserole

2   15-ounce cans cream-style corn

4   eggs

1/2   cup oil

1/2   cup chopped onion

1/2   cup chopped bell peppers

1   6-ounce package jalapeño corn bread mix

1   cup grated cheese

     Salt and pepper to taste

In a 2½-quart round casserole dish combine all of the ingredients. Bake at 400° until golden brown. Cut and serve.

SERVES 5 TO 6.

LaBreeska and Joel Hemphill

Joel and LaBreeska Hemphill pose for a publicity still in 1967, the year of their tenth wedding anniversary.

And three decades later finds them wonderful recording Partners.

Joel and LaBreeska Hemphill

Joel and LaBreeska Hemphill began their ministry and life together as an evangelistic preaching and singing team more than forty years ago when they married on June 28, 1957. They first met when LaBreeska was traveling with Howard, Vestal, and Rusty Goodman doing revival work.

Nine years later, in 1966, Joel and LaBreeska signed with Marvin Norcross to make their first duet recording, an album titled *The Country Style of Joel and LaBreeska Hemphill*. Their second album included the song "Pity the Man," and, just like that, the Hemphills had their first Dove nomination.

Later Tim and Dixie McKeithen made the Hemphill twosome a quartet, but The Hemphills, which most of the gospel music-loving world came to know and love, didn't reach full bloom until Joel and LaBreeska's children, Joey, Trent, and Candy, joined their mom and dad between 1974 and 1990. The five Hemphills became one of the foremost mixed groups in gospel music, and in the meantime Joel was churning out the hits and winning honors for his songwriting gifts.

The Hemphills won six Dove Awards, while Joel was nominated ten times by the Gospel Music Association as songwriter of the year. He has had more than 300 of his songs recorded, not just by family but by such artists as Charlie Daniels, The Gaither Vocal Band, The Cathedrals, and J.D. Sumner and the Stamps Quartet.

In 1990 the three Hemphill children decided to pursue personal interests and start their own families, thus the group disbanded and Joel and LaBreeska became a duet, just as they began.

The Nashville, Tennessee, residents have ministered for thirty years, including ten years of pastoral work in Bastrop, Louisiana. The Hemphills have recorded about thirty albums and have had an abundance of Number One and Top Ten hits,

The Hemphill family treated Nashville-based Baptist Hospital president David Stringfield with a chorus of Christmas carols at Baptist's executive offices in December 1997. Standing, left to right, are Hemphills Sue Ann, Joey, and Trent, David Stringfield, Candy Hemphill-Christmas, Kent Christmas, and Bethni Hemphill. Seated are LaBreeska and Joel Hemphill.

including "He's Still Workin' on Me," "I'm in this Church," "Master of the Wind," "Consider the Lilies", "I Claim the Blood," "The Only Real Peace," "Paid in Full," "Let's Have a Revival," and "Partners in Emotion."

Says the husband-and-wife team, "We love being out there. We're glad people know we are still together, still loving one another, and still loving the Lord."

Today, when not performing or songwriting, Joel and LaBreeska find their favorite pastime is spending time at home with their grandchildren Jasmine, Nicholas, Taylor, Sara-Kate, Madeleine, and William.

Peace in the Valley Pan-Fried Field Corn

12   *ears of field corn, cleaned and silked*
      Bacon drippings
      Salt and pepper to taste

Cream the corn with a corn cutter. Place the corn in large skillet and add enough water to make it soupy. Add bacon grease. Cook over low heat, stirring occasionally to keep the corn from sticking to the bottom of the pan. Add salt and pepper and continue to cook and stir until the corn thickens and starts to bubble and becomes glazed looking. Serve hot.

SERVES 10.

Mr. and Mrs. Les Beasley

Les Beasley sees the "Possum-bilities" with country music legend George Jones, at a taping of The Nashville Network's Prime Time Country.

Florida Boys Fried Corn

6   *to 10 ears corn*
      Oil or bacon drippings
      Water
¼   *cup (½ stick) margarine*
      Salt and pepper to taste

Wash the corn well with a vegetable brush. With a sharp knife, shave off the tops of the kernels and scrape the cobs well. In a large skillet over low heat, pour enough oil to cover the bottom of the skillet. (Be careful not to let the oil get too hot or the corn will stick.) Pour the corn in the skillet, stirring almost constantly to keep the corn from sticking. Then add enough water for the consistency you like, margarine, salt, and pepper. Cook over low heat about 45 minutes to 1 hour until tender.

SERVES 6 TO 8.

Glen Allred • The Florida Boys

Favorite Fried Corn

8	ears fresh corn (white or yellow)
1	medium onion, chopped
3	slices bacon and bacon grease
¼	cup butter
¾	cup water
1	teaspoon salt
½	teaspoon pepper

Remove the husks and silk from the corn. Cut the corn from the cobs, scraping the cobs to remove all of the milk. Add the onion to the corn. In a skillet fry the bacon until crisp. Chop the bacon into pieces and return to the grease. Add the butter. Add the corn mixture to the skillet mixture. Add the water, salt, and pepper. Heat until the mixture comes to a boil. Cover, reduce the heat, and simmer, stirring frequently, for 10 to 12 minutes or until most of the liquid has been absorbed.

SERVES 8.

Ina and Jerry Goff

Jerry Goff is known as Mr. Gospel Trumpet.

Victory Vegetable Casserole

2	to 3 green bell peppers, thinly sliced
1	10-ounce package frozen green beans
1	10-ounce package frozen green peas
1	10-ounce package frozen baby lima beans
1	pint whipping cream
1	cup mayonnaise
1¾	cups Parmesan cheese
	Salt and pepper to taste

Parboil the peppers. Prepare the green beans, peas, and lima beans according to the package instructions. Arrange the vegetables in layers in a 2½-quart baking pan or casserole dish. In a medium bowl combine the whipping cream, mayonnaise, Parmesan cheese, salt, and pepper. Pour over the vegetables. Bake at 350° for 30 to 40 minutes.

SERVES 6.

The Easter Brothers

DOVE SINGLES
Match the artist with their Dove Award-winning song:

1.	The Talleys	A.	"There Rose a Lamb"
2.	The Cathedrals	B.	"I Bowed on My Knees"
3.	The Gaither Vocal Band	C.	"He Is Here"
4.	Gold City	D.	"Out of His Great Love"
5.	The Martins	E.	"Champion of Love"

Answers
1. C 2. E 3. B 4. A 5. D

Joyce's Vegetable Casserole

Casserole:

1   15-ounce can whole-kernel white corn

1   15-ounce can French-style green beans

½   cup chopped celery

¼   cup chopped green bell pepper

1   teaspoon salt

1   teaspoon black pepper

½   cup sour cream

1   10¾-ounce can celery soup

Topping:

1   sleeve Ritz crackers, crushed

½   cup (1 stick) butter, melted

1   2-ounce package almond slices

Drain the juices from the canned vegetables. In a large bowl mix together the corn, green beans, celery, bell pepper, salt, pepper, sour cream, and celery soup. Transfer to a 9 x 13-inch baking dish.

Combine the crackers, butter, and almond slices, and place on top of the casserole mixture. Bake at 350° for 45 minutes.

SERVES ABOUT 8.

Joyce Brown • The Browns

The Browns. Left to right are Joyce Brown, Beecher Brown, Rhonda England, Gary Buckner, and Sharon Sevier.

Hoppers Sweet Potato Casserole

3	cups sweet potatoes, cooked and mashed
1	cup sugar
½	teaspoon salt
3	eggs, beaten
½	cup (1 stick) margarine
½	cup milk
½	teaspoon vanilla extract

Topping:

1	cup firmly packed brown sugar
½	cup all-purpose flour
2½	tablespoons margarine
1	cup chopped nuts

In a mixing bowl beat together the sweet potatoes, sugar, salt, eggs, margarine, milk, and vanilla. Transfer to a 1½-quart casserole dish.

Mix all of the topping ingredients and spoon on top of the potato mixture. Bake at 350° for 35 minutes.

SERVES 6.

Kim Greene Hopper • The Hoppers

The Hoppers began performing more than thirty years ago. Connie has twice been named queen of gospel music by The Singing News. *Their song "Here I Am" stayed at Number One for four consecutive months in 1990. From left to right are Mike Hopper, Shannon Childress, Claude Hopper, Connie Hopper, Kim Greene-Hopper, and Dean Hopper.*

The Hoppers

The Hoppers originated as a family gospel group more than thirty years ago when Claude Hopper and four of his brothers began blending their voices to share the gospel message, while Connie, Claude's wife-to-be, played the piano. They made their first record in a carport.

Today the group includes Claude and Connie; their sons Dean (lead singer) and Michael (drummer); Dean's wife, Kim Greene (soprano); Shannon Childress (pianist); and Frank Mills (bass). In 1983 the Hoppers were named the Top Mixed Group by the Southern Gospel Music Association.

Connie has twice received *The Singing News* Queen of Gospel Music Award and she has also been recognized as the People's Choice Award winner for Gospel Music Female Vocalist of the Year.

Dean is an accomplished musician and has been nominated for *The Singing News* Favorite Lead Singer, while Kim Greene, was selected favorite Young Artist by readers of *The Singing News* in 1990. Michael has been playing drums since age thirteen.

Pianist Shannon Childress also sings and has written several hits for the group, including the Number One tune, "Milk & Honey."

The Hoppers' 1990 hit "Here I Am" stuck to the top of the charts for four straight months and they have since followed with numerous other Number One hits.

The Hoppers are all smiles in this group portrait. Clockwise from top left are Shannon Childress, Dean Hopper, Claude Hopper, Connie Hopper, Mike Hopper, and Kim Greene Hopper.

Swell Sweet Potato Casserole

3	cups cooked mashed sweet potatoes (see note below)
1	cup sugar
2	eggs
½	cup milk
¼	cup (½ stick) margarine (do not use butter—makes it too greasy)
1	teaspoon vanilla butter and nut flavoring (McCormick has this flavor)
½	teaspoon salt

Topping:

½	cup (1 stick) margarine
1	cup firmly packed brown sugar
½	cup all-purpose flour
1	cup chopped pecans

In a medium bowl mix the sweet potatoes, sugar, eggs, milk, margarine, flavoring, and salt until well blended. Transfer to a 9 x 13-inch casserole dish.

In a small saucepan melt the margarine. Stir in the brown sugar. Add the flour and nuts until crumbly. Sprinkle over the sweet potatoes. Bake at 300° for 30 minutes.

Note: Boil the sweet potatoes until done. They're done if a fork stuck in them goes through easily. Mash the potatoes in a mixer, stopping several times to take off the strings that stick to the beater and throw the strings away.

SERVES 8.

The Booth Brothers

Sweet By and By Creamed Sweet Potatoes

5	*pounds sweet potatoes*
¼	*cup (½ stick) margarine*
	Cream

Caramel Sauce:

½	*cup (1 stick) margarine*
2	*cups firmly packed light brown sugar*
1	*cup chopped nuts*

In a large pot, boil the sweet potatoes. Peel and mash them. Add ¼ cup of margarine and just enough cream to thin it a little. Pour into a casserole dish.

In saucepan combine ½ cup of margarine and the brown sugar. Cook over low heat until sugar melts and the sauce is a medium thickness. Pour over the potatoes and sprinkle with the chopped nuts. Bake at 350° for 30 to 40 minutes.

SERVES 8.

Hazel (Mrs. Henry) Slaughter

Henry Slaughter, a five-time Dove Award winner, plays an inspirational medley on the piano for the Sunday Mornin' Country event at the Grand Ole Opry House in 1989.

Sweet Potato Deluxe

2   cups mashed, cooked sweet potatoes

2   eggs

6   tablespoons butter

1¼   cups sugar

½   cup milk

½   teaspoon ground cinnamon

½   teaspoon grated nutmeg

Topping:

½   cup firmly packed light brown sugar

½   cup self-rising flour

1   cup pecans, broken

½   cup melted butter

In a medium bowl mix together the sweet potatoes, eggs, butter, sugar, milk, cinnamon, and nutmeg. Pour the mixture into a greased 9 x 13-inch casserole dish.

In a small bowl combine the brown sugar, flour, pecans, and melted butter, and spoon on top of the sweet potato mixture. Bake at 350° for 20 minutes.

Linda and Roy Fox • The Fox Brothers

Crispy Potato Wedges

4	medium russet potatoes, cut into large wedges
1	tablespoon vegetable oil
⅛	teaspoon salt
¼	teaspoon freshly ground pepper
2	cloves garlic, minced (optional)
	Ketchup

Place the potatoes in a large bowl, and cover with cold water. Let stand for 15 minutes. Preheat the oven to 425°. Spray a nonstick baking sheet with vegetable cooking spray. Set aside.

Drain the potatoes in a colander. Spread the wedges on a double layer of paper towels. Cover with a second layer of paper towels. Press down on the towels to dry the potatoes. Transfer the potatoes to a clean large bowl. Sprinkle with the oil, salt, and pepper. Toss gently to combine. Arrange the seasoned potatoes in a single layer on the prepared baking sheet.

Bake the potatoes for 20 minutes. Using a spatula, turn the potatoes. Sprinkle with garlic. Bake about 20 more minutes until golden, turning the baking sheet after 10 minutes for even browning. Serve immediately with ketchup on the side.

SERVES 4.

Joyce Martin McCollough • The Martins

The Martins serve up wonderful sibling harmonies and, like Abraham Lincoln, spent their early years growing up in a log cabin. Left to right are Jonathan Martin, Joyce Martin McCollough, and Judy Martin Hess.

Here and After Hash Brown Casserole

1	24-ounce package frozen, shredded hash brown potatoes
2	tablespoons butter
1	medium onion, chopped
1	10¾-ounce can cream of chicken or cream of mushroom soup
1	pint sour cream
2	cups grated sharp cheese
¼	cup (½ stick) margarine
	Salt and pepper to taste

Thaw the hash browns 30 minutes before using.

In a small skillet melt the butter and saute the onion until tender. In a large bowl combine all of the ingredients. Transfer to a 9 x 13-inch baking dish. Bake at 350° for 45 minutes to 1 hour.

MAKES 8 SERVINGS.

Fay Shedd • Artist Direction Agency

Shoestring Potato Casserole Beasley

3	pounds shoestring hash browns, thawed
1	onion, chopped
1	10¾-ounce can cream of mushroom soup
1	pint sour cream
	Sharp Cheddar cheese, grated
½	cup (1 stick) margarine, melted
1	cup crushed corn flakes

In a large bowl mix the hash browns, onion, soup, and sour cream, and transfer to a greased 2-quart casserole dish. Top with the cheese. Combine the margarine and corn flakes to make a topping, and spread over the cheese. Bake at 350° until brown.

SERVES 6 TO 8.

Mr. and Mrs. Les Beasley

Down Home Hash Brown Casserole

I love to cook, and most of my stuff turns out just fine. But in the beginning, it was risky to say the least. My mother is the greatest "from scratch" biscuit maker in the world. I thought that talent would just rub off on me naturally, I guess. So when my new boyfriend, Paul Downing, said he loved homemade biscuits on our second or third date, what was I to do? I had made them a few times while still living at home and with my mom overseeing the procedure.

So, I proceeded to bake biscuits to go with the country ham I had bought just for the special occasion of a breakfast for Paul and me as we were getting acquainted. I didn't know that my roommates didn't use self-rising flour, so just use your imagination as to the biscuits made with plain flour—no soda or salt added! We had invited our friend Linda Robinson to have breakfast with us at Linda's and my apartment. She and Paul had a wonderful time pitching the biscuits around the kitchen and living room—once almost knocking a hole in a wall when a biscuit missed its target. I don't know whether I ever convinced them that it was the flour or not, but it was a memory forever etched in my mind. It still brings a laugh!

1	*32-ounce package frozen hashbrown potatoes, thawed*
1	*cup chopped onion, sautéed in butter*
1	*pint sour cream*
1	*10¾-ounce can cream of mushroom soup*
2	*cups grated cheese*
1	*to 2 cups crushed corn flakes or crushed saltines*

In a large bowl combine the hash browns, onion, sour cream, soup, and cheese. Transfer to a 9 x 13-inch casserole dish. Top with the corn flakes. Bake at 350° for 45 minutes to 1 hour.

SERVES 8.

Ann Downing

Paul and Ann Downing (in 1971) toured for more than twenty years and recorded more than forty albums as The Downings.

Twice-As-Nice Potato

It's not low-fat dish, but it's well worth the calories

2	*large russet potatoes, prebaked*
¼	*cup milk*
¼	*cup (½ stick) butter or margarine*
1½	*cups grated Swiss cheese*
2	*tablespoons sour cream*
2	*cups sliced mushrooms*
½	*cup Worcestershire sauce*
	Salt
	Finely chopped chives (optional)

Take the 2 large prebaked potatoes right out of the oven and slice in half lengthwise. Scoop out the insides of both potatoes, and 2 halves as ½-inch thick shells. (The other two shells will not be used. Combine the insides of the potatoes with ¼ stick of the butter or margarine and the sour cream. Mix until smooth. Add the milk to get the potato mixture to a nice creamy consistency. Add salt to taste. Mix in about ¾ cup of the Swiss cheese. Scoop the mixture back into the 2 potato shell halves. Top with the remaining Swiss cheese. Bake at 350° for 10 to 20 minutes. The object is to melt the cheese on top and inside of the potato. Check often to make sure the top doesn't scorch.

On the stovetop, sauté the sliced mushrooms with the remaining ¼ stick of butter or margarine, the Worcestershire sauce, and salt to taste. After you take the potatoes out of the oven, place each on a serving dish and top with the sautéed mushrooms. Sprinkle the top with freshly chopped chives for more taste and color.

MAKE 2 MEAL-SIZED SERVINGS.

Pamela Stansberry • The Gospel Voice

The Gospel Voice

The Gospel Voice Magazine is a monthly publication that contains feature stories and news about the world of Southern Gospel music.

It was originally formed in 1987 as a gospel music trade and industry publication. In the late 1980s *The Gospel Voice* was promoted on The Nashville Network during the popular television show *Gospel Jubilee* and quickly began building an international fan base of subscribers.

Recently the magazine was purchased by Gottem Entertainment and has been greatly expanded to include more fan related feature stories and information that makes it much more entertaining, while remaining one of the industry's leading publications for Southern Gospel.

The Gospel Voice offers in-depth feature stories, a monthly Top 80 radio singles chart, a Top 20 Christian country chart, industry news columns, fan news columns, artists' tour routes, album reviews, Christian book reviews, industry leaders profiles, video reviews, and more.

In addition to these features, *The Gospel Voice* gives its readers the opportunity to vote each year in the annual *Gospel Voice* Diamond Awards, which has become one of gospel music's most respected and prestigious awards. The awards are presented each year in a ceremony held during the Southern Gospel Music Fest held each June at the Municipal

Pamela Stansberry, managing editor of The Gospel Voice.

Auditorium in Nashville.

For more information on receiving *The Gospel Voice,* call (615) 851-1841 or write to 515 Two Mile Parkway, Suite 212, Goodlettsville, TN, 37072-2025.

THEY'RE NUMBER ONE

Match the gospel artists with their Number One hit on the Singing News Chart:

1.	The Cathedrals	A.	"I Got Up and Went"
2.	The Bishops	B.	"He's Still in the Fire"
3.	The Florida Boys	C.	"The Blood Is Still There"
4.	Jerry and The Goffs	D.	"Anchor to the Power of the Cross"
5.	The Freemans	E.	"Jesus Is Mine"
6.	The Hemphills	F.	"From the Depths of My Heart"
7.	The Greenes	G.	"I Will Rise Up From the Grave"
8.	The New Hinsons	H.	"I'm Going Home With Jesus"
9.	The Nelons	I.	"Arise"
10.	The McKameys	J.	"I'm Glad I Know Who Jesus Is"
11.	The McGruders	K.	"Old Ship of Zion"
12.	The Kingsmen	L.	"He's My Hiding Place"
13.	The Isaacs	M.	"Wedding Music"
14.	The Inspirations	N.	"I Lean on You Lord"
15.	The Hoppers	O.	"Hello in Heaven"
16.	The Speers	P.	"Please Search the Book Again"
17.	The Kevin Spencer Family	Q.	"Jesus' Rocking Chair"
18.	The Steeles	R.	"It Wasn't Raining (When Noah Built the Ark)"

Answers
1. M, 2. L, 3. N, 4. P, 5. O, 6. R, 7. Q, 8. K, 9. J, 10. I, 11. H, 12. G, 13. F, 14. E, 15. D, 16. B, 17. C, 18. A.

BREAKFASTS

Saw the Light Sausage Casserole

1	pound ground sausage, crumbled and cooked
2	cups grated Cheddar cheese
1	cup Bisquick
4	eggs
1	cup milk

Butter a 9 x 13-inch casserole dish. Layer the sausage and then the cheese in the dish. In a blender mix the milk, eggs, and Bisquick. Pour the mixture over the sausage and cheese. Bake at 350° for 30 to 35 minutes. May be frozen and cooked later.

SERVES 8 TO 9.

The Kingdom Heirs

Let the Little Things Go Sausage Roll

This is our annual Christmas breakfast. We make it Christmas Eve and refrigerate it. Then we slice and bake it on Christmas Day. The kids love it!

1	*pound sausage*
2	*cups self-rising flour*
1	*8-ounce package cream cheese*
½	*cup (1 stick) butter*

In a skillet cook the sausage. Drain. In a large bowl combine the remaining ingredients to form a dough. Roll the dough out and then sprinkle with the sausage, and roll up the dough. Refrigerate. Slice into 1-inch wide pieces. Bake at 450° for 12 to 15 minutes.

SERVES 4 TO 6.

Jeff and Sheri Easter

Jeff and Sheri Easter combine the pleasing sounds of bluegrass along with their Southern gospel harmonies. Says Jeff, "We're not any category ... we're just Jeff and Sheri." Left to right are Greg Ritchie, Jeff and Sheri Easter, and Rabbit Easter.

Jeff and Sheri Easter

One of Southern Gospel's most favored duos comes by its musical abilities honestly. The husband-and-wife combination of Jeff and Sheri Easter have the music in their bloodlines.

Jeff is son of James Easter of The Easter Brothers, and Sheri's mother is a sister of The Lewis Family. And, coincidentally, says Sheri, "The day I was born, my father performed on the radio with The Easter Brothers."

Sheri became a full-time member of The Lewis Family when she finished college. She and Jeff met at the Albert E. Brumley Gospel Sing in Springdale, Arkansas, in 1984 and wed on June 18, 1985. After their marriage, the couple performed with The Lewis Family. Since the late 1980s and into the 1990s, Jeff and Sheri have come into their own. During the '90s they have had more than fifteen Top Twenty songs and have been nominated for eight Dove awards and a Grammy. They were named *The Singing News* gospel duo of the year in 1989.

Their album *Thread of Hope* was named album of the year and the title song received song of the year from the 1995 Hearts Aflame Awards, while the single was also song of the year from *The Gospel Voice*. In 1996 Jeff and Sheri received the Hearts Aflame Award for best video with "Let the Little Things Go," which was also named Christian country song of the year by *The Gospel Voice*. Then they were named Christian country group of the year in 1996 by *The Gospel Voice*.

Sheri has numerous awards for her vocals. She has been named a Southern Gospel female vocalist of the year by *Cash Box,* and for three years was named contemporary female vocalist of the year by the Society of the Preservation of Bluegrass Music in America. Sheri has been favorite female vocalist by *The Gospel Voice* six times and was selected favorite Southern Gospel female vocalist in 1995 and 1996 by *The Singing News*.

Jeff and Sheri keep the family in their act. Jeff's brother, Steve "Rabbit" Easter, plays steel guitar, banjo, and Dobro for the group, while their son, Madison, sometimes will pop on stage to fiddle around and recite Bible verses. Daughter Morgan will hit a few notes on the harmonica.

The Easters reside in Lincolnton, Georgia, where they have a recording studio in their home.

Egg 'em on Egg Bake

1	pound sausage
8	large or 10 medium eggs, slightly beaten
1	cup milk
1	cup shredded sharp cheese
1	tablespoon yellow mustard
2	cups cubed bread or breadcrumbs
	Salt and pepper to taste

In a skillet cook the sausage. Drain. Pour the lightly beaten eggs into a large mixing bowl. Stir in the remaining ingredients, including the cooked sausage. Do not stir hard; just mix slightly. Pour into a greased casserole dish. Bake at 350° for 30 to 45 minutes, checking for over-cooking or dryness. Serve hot.

SERVES 6.

Lou Wills Hildreth

The Wills Family

Lou Wills Hildreth worked with a talent agency in Nashville for many years. Today she especially enjoys the fellowship around the sumptuous meals served by Bill and Gloria Gaither to the cast of their Gaither Homecoming Video Series.

Alabama Breakfast Soufflé

Great for brunch!

3 tablespoons butter

6 slices bread, crusts removed

1 pound pork sausage, cooked, crumbled, and drained

1½ cups grated Cheddar cheese

5 eggs

1 10-ounce can evaporated milk

1 teaspoon salt

1 heaping teaspoon dry mustard

Butter the bread and cut into cubes. Place in a 9 x 13-inch baking dish. Sprinkle with the sausage. Top with the cheese. In a medium bowl beat the remaining ingredients together and pour over the sausage mixture. Chill overnight.

Bake uncovered at 350° for 40 to 45 minutes. Serve with fruit.

SERVES 6 TO 8.

Gail (Mrs. Jack) Toney • The Statesmen

Gail and Jack Toney enjoy the afterglow of a good meal with friend Nancy Carswell.

The National Quartet Convention

In September 1997 in Louisville, Kentucky, The National Quartet Convention (NQC) celebrated its fortieth anniversary.

The annual event displays the finest acts in Southern Gospel music and features more than seventy groups entertaining over a period of six days and nights.

When J.D. Sumner began the National Quartet Convention in 1957, Southern Gospel fans hoped that it would prove popular enough to turn into an annual festival. It has done not only that but now attracts tens of thousands of gospel music lovers.

"The size and scope of the anniversary of the National Quartet Convention is a testament to the vision of the founders and the administrative abilities of its current owners," says Clarke Beasley, executive director of the NQC.

Recalls Eldridge Fox, whose Kingsmen Quartet was just getting its professional feet wet during the first few years of the convention, "It was the epitome of all gospel music. For groups like us who were just getting into the business, the aura of all that talent was overwhelming. The quartet convention was the greatest thing that ever happened in our business. The amount of togetherness it generated among the groups had never before been equaled and never has since."

The NQC started in Memphis, Tennessee, when the three-day event brought in about five thousand Southern Gospel musicians and fans. As the convention grew, organizers moved the event to Nashville in 1971. After twenty-two years in Music City, they moved again, this time to its current home in Louisville, Kentucky.

The first NQC in Louisville in 1994 drew record numbers of people to the Kentucky Fair and Exposi-tion Center. More than eighteen thousand fans showed up for a Friday night

The inspiring scene at the 1997 National Quartet Convention in Louisville, Kentucky.

performance, the largest group for which many artists had ever performed.

"There are many people who've been coming since the first one and stay all six days and nights," says Les Beasley, lead singer and manager of The Florida Boys and long-time convention performer. "The convention continues to grow, and it will as long as we give the people what they want."

Clarke Beasley believes the convention won't stop growing, at least any time soon. "It's exciting to know that gospel music's biggest event is still growing by astounding rates," he says.

The convention is not just about performances, however. Attendees get the chance to experience a 120,000 square-foot exhibition hall filled with booths and exhibits. People can meet their favorite performers, take part in special events, and see some of the industry business going on as well. Professionals are able to take the opportunity to listen to industry speakers, attend seminars and catch up on all the latest Southern Gospel information.

Clarke Beasley, who was appointed executive director by the board of directors of NQC in 1993, is responsible for launching a West Coast version of the NQC. The original Great Western Quartet Convention occurred in May 1997 in Fresno, California, and gave many music lovers their first look at Southern Gospel music.

Very Toney Breakfast Danish

- 2   8-roll cans refrigerator crescent rolls
- 2   8-ounce packages cream cheese
- ¾   cup sugar
- 1   egg, separated
- 1   teaspoon vanilla extract
- 1   tablespoon lemon juice

Glaze:

- 1½   cups confectioners' sugar
- 1   tablespoon butter
- 1   teaspoon vanilla extract
- Lemon juice to taste

Unroll 1 can of the crescent rolls and place them flat over the bottom of a 9 x 13-inch baking dish. In a medium bowl mix the cream cheese, sugar, egg yolk, vanilla, and lemon juice, and spread on top of the rolls. Unroll the second can of rolls and place flat on top. Beat the egg white until foamy and spread on top. Bake at 350° for 20 minutes.

In a small bowl combine the confectioners' sugar, butter, vanilla, and lemon juice to taste. Spread the glaze while the dish is still hot.

SERVES 6 TO 8.

Gail (Mrs. Jack) Toney • The Statesmen

Wherever You Are French Toast

1	large egg
2	egg whites
¼	cup milk
½	teaspoon vanilla extract
½	teaspoon ground cinnamon
⅛	teaspoon grated nutmeg (optional)
8	1-inch-thick, diagonally-cut slices French or Italian bread
	Cinnamon sugar and maple syrup

In a shallow bowl using a wire whisk or a fork beat the egg and egg whites until foamy. Add the milk, vanilla, cinnamon, and nutmeg. Beat well and set aside.

Preheat the oven to 200°. Lightly spray a nonstick skillet with vegetable spray and place over medium heat. Dip 4 slices of the bread into the egg mixture, turning to coat and draining the excess back into the dish. Place the bread slices into the prepared skillet. Cook until golden brown, turning once, about 1 or 2 minutes per slice. Transfer the cooked slices to a plate, and keep warm in the oven. Dip the remaining slices into the egg mixture, and cook the same way as the first batch.

Divide the French toast slices among the serving plates. Sprinkle lightly with cinnamon sugar and maple syrup. Serve immediately.

SERVES 4.

Milinda and Jonathan Martin • The Martins

The Martins in the early stages of their career.

The Martins

The brother and sisters trio of The Martins has brought one of the freshest as well as hottest new sounds to Southern Gospel music in recent years.

Joyce, Jonathan, and Judy have been singing together since childhood. The siblings were raised most of their lives in a cabin with no electricity or running water outside of Hamburg, Arkansas, where their father was a crop-duster pilot.

Heavily influenced by the music of The Rambos and The Messengers, The Martins originally recorded for Mark V Records, but now make music for Spring Hill. After meeting Bill Gaither and being invited to perform on The Gaithers' Precious Memories video, their career has taken a huge upswing.

The trio captured two Dove awards in 1996, for Southern Gospel album of the year *(The Martins)* and Southern Gospel song of the year ("Out of His Great Love"), and repeated in the same two categories in 1997 with "Wherever You Are" and "Only God Knows," respectively. They have twice been named trio of the year by the *Gospel Voice* Diamond Voice Awards (1995 and 1996), and were selected as artist of the year by the Hearts Aflame Awards in 1997. The sibling singers have also proven their versatility with *An A Capella Hymns Collection*.

"We find success in variety on the stage, and that is what appeals to us and to a lot of people who come to hear us sing. We also have a stronger message in Southern Gospel," says Joyce Martin.

"We really want to have a strong message; that is a big thing with us. I don't have any conviction I can force on anybody else. But we feel strongly about what we sing.

The Martins a few years ago: Joyce (top), Judy, and Jonathan.

"We have always been a group that speaks more to the Christian, a person raised in church. It's easier for us to identify with that person because we were raised in the church, and we make it clear what our evangelistic message is. We are more appealing to the person who is born again and struggling to either walk that walk or in witnessing or living their life."

Judy, incidentally, is married to Jake Hess Jr. Joyce is married to Harry McCollough, and Jonathan's wife is Milinda.

Kevin's Pancakes

I call these Kevin's Pancakes because this was the first thing I cooked for him when we got back from our honeymoon. After that, he wanted them every morning for breakfast. He loves to spread peanut butter over them and then pour the syrup on.

1	*egg*
1	*cup all-purpose flour*
¾	*cup milk*
2	*tablespoons vegetable oil*
1	*tablespoon sugar*
3	*teaspoons baking powder*
½	*teaspoon salt*
	Butter

In a mixing bowl beat the egg with a hand beater until fluffy. Beat in the next 6 ingredients just until smooth. (For smoother pancakes, add an additional ¼ cup of milk.) In an electric skillet or griddle melt the butter and then pour the batter by the spoonful or from a pitcher to make individual pancakes the size you like them. Cook the pancakes until puffed and dry around the edges, and then turn them over until the other sides are golden brown.

MAKES ABOUT SIX 4-INCH PANCAKES

The Kevin Spencer Family

The Kevin Spencer Family is a trio from Jonesboro, Arkansas, composed of husband and wife Kevin and Tammy Spencer and Brian Monchan. The group has been named The Singing News *Horizon Group of the Year and* Gospel Voice *Sunrise Group of the Year. Kevin wrote* The Singing News *Number One song of the year in 1991, "Let's Meet by the River." He is also known for "It'll Be Worth It After All" and "Shepherd of My Valley."*

❧ DESSERTS ☙

Preserving a Husband

Be careful in your selection. Do not choose too young and take only such as have been reared in a good, moral atmosphere. Some insist on keeping them in a pickle, while others keep them in hot water. This only makes them sour, hard, and bitter. Even the poor variety may be sweet, tender, and good by garnishing them with patience, well sweetened with smiles, and flavored with kisses to taste. Then wrap them in a mantle for charity, keep them warm with a steady fire of domestic devotion, and serve with three good meals a day. When thus prepared, they will keep for years.

Ora Blanch (Mrs. Martin) Cook • The Inspirations

Those inducted into the Southern Gospel Music Association
Hall of Fame in May of 1997 included, left to right, Les Beasley, Rita
McDuffie (daughter of Wendy Bagwell), J.G. Whitfield, Mosie Lister. J.D. Sumner,
James Blackwood, Glen Payne, Eva Mae LeFevre, Bill Gaither, Brock Speer, Jake Hess
and Hovie Lister. Governor Jimmie Davis and Dottie Rambo were the only two artists
inducted into the "Living" category who could not be present.

Scripture Cake

1.) $4\frac{1}{2}$ cups I Kings 4:22

2.)   1 cup Judges 5:25

3.)   2 cups Jeremiah 6:20

4.)   2 cups I Samuel 30:12

5.)   2 cups Nahum 3:12

6.)   2 cups Numbers 17:8

7.)   2 tablespoons I Samuel 14:24

8.)   1 pinch Leviticus 2:13

9.) $\frac{1}{2}$ dozen Jeremiah 17:11

10.) $\frac{1}{2}$ cup Judges 4:19

11.)   **Seasoning II Chronicles 9:9**

Follow the directions of Solomon for bringing up a child; Proverbs 23:14. Bake as a loaf cake in a preheated 325° oven for about 50 minutes.

     Note: All references are according to King James version.

     1.) Self-rising flour; 2.) butter; 3.) sugar; 4.) raisins; 5.) figs; 6.) almonds; 7.) honey; 8.) salt; 9.) eggs; 10.) milk; 11.) your favorite seasonings (vanilla, cinnamon).

Ora Blanch and Martin Cook • The Inspirations

Another Reading of Scripture Cake

1	cup Judges 5:25; last clause (butter)
2	cups Jeremiah 6:20 (sugar)
2	teaspoons I Samuel 14:25; last clause (honey)
6	Jeremiah 17:11 (eggs)
½	cup Judges 4:19; last clause (milk)
4½	cups I Kings 4:22 (all-purpose flour)
2	teaspoons Amos 4:5 (baking powder)
1	cup I Samuel 30:12; 2nd phrase (raisins)
1	cup Nahum 3:12 (figs)
	II Chronicles 9:9 (spices of choice)

Grease a tube pan. In a large bowl cream together the butter, sugar, and honey. In a medium bowl beat the eggs until frothy. Add the milk to the eggs. Add the egg mixture to the creamed mixture and beat thoroughly. In a separate bowl sift together the flour and baking powder. Add the dry ingredients to the creamed mixture, mixing well. Chop the raisins and figs and add to the mixture. Add spices as desired. Pour the batter into the prepared pan. Bake at 375° for about 30 minutes.

SERVES 10.

The Cumberland Boys

The Cumberland Boys take advantage of a Pennsylvania restaurant that serves up whopping-sized pancakes while they're on the road.

The Cumberland Boys began in 1980 at Opryland when they were organized by Bob Whittaker, now manager of the Grand Ole Opry. Since then the quartet has performed an average of four shows a day, six day a week before millions of people. Left to right are baritone Bill Britt, tenor Depp Britt, bass singer Steve Goforth, and lead singer Jim Worthing.

Ring the Bells Uncooked Fruitcake

1	cup (2 sticks) margarine
1	16-ounce bag marshmallows
1	16-ounce package graham crackers, crushed
1	teaspoon grated nutmeg
1	6-ounce bottle maraschino cherries
1	quart pecans, broken
1	3½-ounce can shredded coconut
1	6-ounce package mixed candied fruit (optional)

Line a 1½-quart pan with waxed paper. In a large saucepan melt the margarine and marshmallows together. Mix the remaining ingredients and blend into the marshmallow mixture. Mix well. Turn into the prepared pan. Store in a cool place.

SERVES 10 TO 12.

Candy Hemphill-Christmas

One of the many popular family groups of the 1970s and '80s was The Hemphills, headed by Joel and LaBreeska Hemphill. Joel is a prolific songwriter and for the group penned such numbers as "He's Still Working on Me," "I'm in this Church," "Master of the Wind," "It Wasn't Raining When Noah Built the Ark," and "Consider the Lilies." Clockwise from top left in a 1984 photograph are Candy, Trent, Joey, LaBreeska, and Joel Hemphill.

Foxy's Graham Cracker Cake

2   cups sugar

1   cup (2 sticks) margarine

5   eggs

1   teaspoon baking powder

2   teaspoons vanilla extract

1   cup flaked coconut

1   cup chopped nuts

1   cup milk

1   16-ounce box graham cracker crumbs

Filling:

½   cup (1 stick) margarine, softened

1   16-ounce box confectioners' sugar

1   20-ounce can crushed pineapple, drained (reserve the juice)

Grease and flour 3 9-inch round cake pans. In a large bowl mix the sugar, margarine, and eggs well. Add the remaining ingredients one at a time, mixing until well blended. Pour into the prepared pans. Bake at 350° for 30 to 35 minutes.

In a medium bowl cream the margarine and mix in the confectioners' sugar a portion at a time. Add the pineapple and mix. Spread between the layers of cake. Pour the reserved pineapple juice over top, if desired.

SERVES 10 TO 12.

Eldridge Fox • The Kingsmen

Grandmother Puckett's Coconut Cake

1	18 ¾-ounce box white cake mix

Icing:

1	tablespoon flour
1	cup sugar
2	cups milk
2	egg whites
1	tablespoon butter
1	fresh coconut, grated, with milk reserved
1	teaspoon vanilla extract

Grease 2 9-inch round cake pans. In a large bowl prepare the cake batter according to the package directions. Pour into the prepared pans. Bake according to the package directions.

In the top of a double boiler mix together the flour, sugar, and milk. In a medium bowl beat the egg whites until stiff, and then fold them into the liquid mixture. Cook over simmering water until the mixture thickens. Remove the pan from the heat and add the butter and vanilla. Reserve enough coconut to sprinkle on the top and sides of the cake, and add the rest to the icing mixture. Allow the icing to cool.

Spread the icing between the cake layers and on the top and sides. Sprinkle coconut on top and pat on the sides. Drizzle the reserved coconut milk on top.

SERVES 10.

Bethni and Trent Hemphill

Trent Hemphill began performing as bass guitarist with his family when he was fifteen. He moved to the piano five years later. As a songwriter, Trent has had songs recorded by The Perrys ("I'm Bound for a City"), The Greenes ("I Know Jesus"), Heirloom ("Send Down Your Glory"), and The Hemphills ("Let the Whole World Know Jesus Saves"). Trent retired from the road in 1990 to spend more time with his family and to focus on his bus leasing business. Bethni Hemphill has worked in Southern Gospel since 1985. She produced the weekly syndicated television show Homeland Harmony. *She also has produced videos, including* The Speers' 75th Anniversary *and* The Cathedrals' Reunion, *which was voted Favorite Southern Gospel Video by* The Singing News *Fan Awards and The Hearts Aflame Awards.*

Quick and Delicious Coconut Cake

- 1   18¾-ounce box super moist butter recipe cake mix
- 1   15-ounce can cream of coconut
- 1   14-ounce can sweetened condensed milk
- 1   large container non-dairy whipped topping
- 2   6-ounce packages frozen shredded coconut, thawed

Preheat the oven to 350°. Prepare the cake batter and bake according to the package directions. Allow the cake to cool. In a medium bowl mix the cream of coconut and the sweetened condensed milk. Make holes in the cake. Pour the mixture over the cake. After the liquid is absorbed, cover the cake with the whipped topping. Spread the shredded coconut over the cake.

You're supposed to refrigerate it for 1 hour, but I don't wait a minute. I eat it quick while it's still warm.

SERVES 10 TO 12.

Little Jan Buckner

Wendy Bagwell and The Sunliters of 1968 were Geraldine Morrison, Bagwell, and Jan Buckner. Bagwell was known as the poet laureate of gospel music and wrote the million-seller "Here Come the Rattlesnakes."

I Don't Want No Rocks Coconut Cream Cake

1   18¾-ounce box yellow cake mix

1   14-ounce can sweetened condensed milk

1   14-ounce can cream of coconut

1   9-ounce carton nondairy whipped topping

1   cup shredded coconut

Grease a 9 x 13-inch pan. In a large bowl mix the cake batter according the package directions. Pour into the prepared pan. Bake at 350° for 30 minutes or until done. Let the cake cool.

Punch holes in the cake with the end of a wooden spoon. Pour the sweetened condensed milk onto the cake. Pour the cream of coconut onto the cake. Top with nondairy whipped topping, and sprinkle with coconut. Enjoy!

SERVES 8 TO 10.

Tammy Underwood • The Perry Sisters

Golden Apricot Nectar Cake

1   18¾-ounce box yellow cake mix

¾   cup vegetable oil

¾   apricot nectar

4   eggs

Glaze:

1½   cups confectioners' sugar

Juice of 2 lemons or ⅓ cup bottled lemon juice

Preheat the oven to 325°. Grease and flour a Bundt or tube pan. In a large bowl beat together the cake mix, oil, apricot nectar, and eggs. Pour the batter into the prepared pan. Bake for 55 minutes.

In a medium bowl combine the confectioners' sugar and lemon juice. Punch holes in the cake using an ice pick. Pour the glaze on the hot cake. Let cool in the pan for 1 to 2 hours before serving.

SERVES 10.

Mark Trammell • Gold City Quartet

Goodman Sour Cream Pound Cake

1   18¾-ounce box white cake mix

½   cup sugar

¾   cup vegetable oil

1   8-ounce container sour cream

4   eggs

2   teaspoons ground cinnamon

3   teaspoons sugar

½   cup nuts

Icing:

1   cup confectioners' sugar

2   tablespoons milk

½   tablespoon vanilla extract

Preheat the oven to 300°. Grease and flour a tube pan. In a large bowl combine the cake mix, sugar, oil, amd sour cream. Add the eggs one at a time, beating after each addition. Pour half of the batter into the tube pan.

In a small bowl mix the cinnamon, sugar, and nuts. Put the nut mixture on the batter in the pan and then add the rest of the batter. Bake for 1 hour. Let cool and remove from pan.

In a saucepan combine the confectioners' sugar, milk, and vanilla, and bring to a boil. Spread over the cooled cake.

SERVES 10.

Billy (Mrs. Rusty) Goodman • The Happy Goodmans

The Happy Goodman Family on TV in the '60s. Left to right are Sam, Vestal, Rusty, Bob, and Howard Goodman.

The Happy Goodman Family

One of the major influences on the Southern Gospel sound, its singers and fans, is that of The Happy Goodman family.

The Happy Goodmans originally featured brothers Howard (lead), Rusty (bass), and Sam (baritone) and Howard's wife, Vestal (soprano). Howard's sisters, Bobby, Stella, and Gussie, also sang with the group through the years. The quartet recorded its first album in the early 1950s and in the ensuing years have returned to the studios for fifty more albums of happy-filled Happy Goodman songs.

The Happy Goodmans were original members of the *Gospel Singing Jubilee* TV show and in 1974 starred in their own *Happy Goodman Family Hour* TV show. During its tenure as one of the most prominent groups in Southern Gospel, the quartet covered hundreds of thousands of miles in a Silver Eagle bus and played thousands of concerts.

The Goodmans grew up near the northern Alabama town of Vinemont but for many years now have made their home in Madisonville, Kentucky, where Howard is minister and pastor of New Life Temple. Howard learned to play the piano as a child and loved to sing. As his younger brothers and sisters came along, he taught each one a certain part, and eventually they became the harmonious Happy Goodman Family.

Until the time of his death, Rusty produced the Goodman albums and was a productive songwriter who penned such classics as "I Wouldn't Take Nothing for My Journey Now" (the Goodmans' theme song), "Had It Not Been (For the Old Rugged Cross)," "Who Am I," and "Until You've Known the Love of God." Rusty also performed with The Plainsmen for over six years, and he co-wrote pop hits such as "North To Alaska."

Since Rusty's death, Johnny Minick, who was with the group for more than twenty years as bass

The all-sibling Happy Goodman Family, appearing on radio WNGO in Wingo, Kentucky, in 1945, are, left to right, Sam, Ruth, Rusty, Gussie, Stella, Eloise, and Howard, on piano.

guitarist, has become a vocalist and keyboardist with The Happy Goodmans.

Vestal began her career singing as a youngster in church. "I was in church all my life and sang all of my life as well. I met Howard when my brother, who was singing some with Howard, came with the Goodmans to sing at a revival near my home in Albertville, Alabama. My mom, dad and I went that night and I met Howard. Four years later we were married and I joined their family as a Happy Goodman."

Vestal and the Goodmans have captured two Grammys and five Dove Awards. Fans know their biggest hits, such as "What a Lovely Name," "God Walks the Dark Hills," "I Don't Regret a Mile," and "I'm Too Near Home to Turn Back Now," by heart.

With that unmistakable alto voice and outstanding range, Vestal recorded her first solo album in 1975. "I've always sung a lot of solos in the concerts we do as a family. I even do some solo concerts now, taking our piano player Johnny Minick with me. It just evolved into solo albums.

"I just like to sing. I can sing anytime, even if it's the first thing I do in the morning," says Vestal, winner of the first Dove Award ever presented by the Gospel Music Association for female vocalist of the year in 1969.

"If I have a goal in gospel music, it would be to inspire young people to become a part of gospel music. I sing for myself because I need to feel God using me, but I sing for others because I want to touch them the way the Lord has touched me through music," says Vestal. "I want my music — our music — to tell folks that yes, we may be in a war, but the battle is the Lord's and the victory is already ours. Praise the Lord!"

Says Mark Lowry, "Vestal is the greatest female gospel singer ever! I call her 'mama,' 'friend,' and the only "Queen of Gospel music."

The gospel songbird has other talents as well. In 1997 she put together a children's video titled *Homecoming Kids Go West*. Incidentally, Vestal is sister to Cat Freeman, who was a first tenor for The Blackwood Brothers Quartet and The Statesmen Quartet for many years.

And Vestal's and Howard's musical abilities have been passed on down through the family. Their son Rick is now contributing songs he has written for The Happy Goodmans.

"Our strength lies in the fact that we believe in what we are doing and we are Christian people. When we sing a gospel song, we sing it from the depth of our heart and soul; it relates to other people whether they are Christian or not because there is a reality to it," says Howard Goodman.

Share the Message Mandarin Orange Cake

1	18¾-ounce box Duncan Hines butter cake mix
4	eggs
½	cup vegetable oil
1	11-ounce can mandarin orange slices with juice

Icing:

1	20-ounce can crushed pineapple with juice
1	16-ounce carton nondairy whipped topping
1	3½-ounce box instant vanilla pudding (do not premix)

Preheat the oven to 350°. Grease 3 8-inch round cake pans. In a large bowl combine the cake mix, eggs oil, and mandarin orange slices and juice. Mix well. Pour the batter into the prepared pans. Bake for 25 minutes.

In a medium bowl combine the pineapple with juice, whipped topping, and pudding. Mix together and beat for 3 to 4 minutes. When the cake is cool, spread the icing between the layers and on top. Keep refrigerated. This recipe is easy but good!

Archie Watkins • The Inspirations

Mary's Spicy Apple Cake

This cake has never lasted longer than 30 minutes, in even the smallest of crowds!

4	*cups diced apples*
2	*eggs*
$\frac{1}{2}$	*cup oil*
2	*cups sugar*
1	*teaspoon vanilla extract*
$\frac{1}{2}$	*teaspoon salt*
1	*heaping teaspoon soda*
$1\frac{1}{2}$	*teaspoons ground cinnamon*
1	*cup walnuts*
2	*cups all-purpose flour*

Glaze:

$\frac{1}{2}$	*cup sugar*
$\frac{1}{2}$	*cup milk*
$1\frac{1}{4}$	*teaspoon butter*

Grease a 9 x 13-inch pan. In a large bowl mix the apples, eggs, oil, sugar, and vanilla. Stir in all the dry ingredients except the nuts and about ¼ cup of the flour. Coat the walnuts with the reserved flour and stir them into the batter. Spread the batter into the prepared pan. Bake at 350° for 1 hour.

Mix the glaze in a saucepan and bring to a boil. When the sugar is dissolved and smooth, pour the glaze over the cake.

SERVES 9 TO 12.

Mary Cleary

Grandma's Apple Cake

This is my mother's famous recipe that everyone insists on her bringing, whether it be family get-togethers or church outings. Yum-yum!

1	*cup vegetable oil*
3	*eggs*
1¾	*cups sugar*
2	*cups self-rising flour*
1	*teaspoon ground cinnamon*
6	*cups diced apples, preferably Macintosh*

Preheat the oven to 350°. Grease a 9 x 13-inch greased baking dish. In a large bowl mix the oil, eggs, and sugar until well blended. Add the flour, cinnamon, and diced apples. Pour into the prepared pan. Bake for 45 minutes or until golden brown.

SERVES 9.

The Kevin Spencer Family

Kevin Spencer (center) celebrates at his Number One party in 1996 with former Gospel Voice *editors Lydia Hardin-Dixon and Rick Francis.*

Apple Dapple Cake

This was Herman's favorite cake.

1½   cups vegetable oil

3   eggs

2   cups sugar

2   teaspoons vanilla extract

3   cups all-purpose flour

1   teaspoon baking soda

1½   teaspoons ground cinnamon

1   cup chopped walnuts

3   cups finely chopped apples

Topping:

½   cup (1 stick) butter

1   cup firmly packed brown sugar

1   cup milk

Jo Harper holds the first annual Heritage Award honoring her late husband, Herman, as their son Ed expresses the family's thanks, while being joined on stage by other Harper sons, Jeff (left) and Clay.

Preheat the oven to 350°. Grease and flour a tube pan. In a large bowl combine the oil, eggs, sugar, and vanilla, and beat until blended. In a separate bowl sift together the flour, soda, and cinnamon. With a wooden spoon stir the dry ingredients into the liquid mixture. Add the chopped nuts and apples to the mixture. Pour into the prepared pan. Bake for 1 hour.

In a saucepan combine the butter, brown sugar and milk, and boil for 2½ minutes. Pour the topping over the cake.

SERVES 10 TO 12.

Jo (Mrs. Herman) Harper • Harper & Associates

Irish Apple Cake

1	cup vegetable oil
2	cups sugar
2	eggs
1	teaspoon vanilla extract
2½	cups all-purpose flour
1	teaspoon salt
2	teaspoons baking powder
1	teaspoon ground cinnamon
4	cups peeled and diced apples
1	cup chopped walnuts
1	12-ounce package butterscotch chips

Preheat the oven to 350°. Grease and flour a 9 x 13-inch pan. In a large bowl beat together the vegetable oil, sugar, eggs, and vanilla. In a separate bowl combine the flour, salt, baking powder, and cinnamon. Add the dry ingredients to the liquid mixture, and mix well. Add the apples. Fold in the nuts. Pour the batter into the prepared pan. Sprinkle butterscotch chips evenly over the top. Do not mix. Bake for 50 to 60 minutes.

SERVES 10.

Debra Talley • The Talley Trio

Out of His Great Love Strawberry Shortcake

1¾   cups all-purpose flour

2   tablespoons sugar

1   tablespoon baking powder

½   teaspoon grated orange peel

3   tablespoons butter or margarine, cut into pieces

¾   cup milk

Filling:

2   pints fresh strawberries, sliced

1   tablespoon orange juice

2   tablespoons sugar

Topping:

    Whipped topping or vanilla yogurt

Preheat the oven to 450°. Spray a baking sheet with vegetable spray. Set aside. In a large bowl sift together the flour, 2 tablespoons sugar, and baking powder. Stir in the orange peel.

In a large bowl cut the butter into the flour mixture using a pastry blender or 2 knives until coarse crumbs form. Quickly stir in the milk until a soft dough forms. On a lightly floured surface, roll out the dough to ½-inch thickness. Using a 2½-inch biscuit cutter, cut out the biscuits. Gather the trimmings, re-roll, and cut out more biscuits. Place on the prepared baking sheet. Bake for 12 to 15 minutes, or until golden brown. Place the biscuits on a wire rack to cool slightly.

To prepare the filling, in a large bowl combine the strawberries, orange juice, and sugar, and mix well. Split the warm biscuits in half horizontally. Place the bottom halves on serving plates. Top each with some filling. Cover with biscuit tops. Serve with the remaining filling. Garnish with whipped topping or yogurt.

SERVES 8.

Judy Martin Hess • The Martins

Love Did Carrot Cake

Seeing new places and meeting new friends are just two of the joys of what we do. Each area of the country has its own taste and cuisine, but my favorite place to eat is at home. No one can put it together and cook like my wife, Shirley. Her home-style carrot cake is one of my favorites. Try it, you'll enjoy it. It will take you home.

2   cups carrots

1   cup chopped pecans

2   cups sugar

1¼ cups vegetable oil

2   teaspoons ground cinnamon

4   egg whites, beaten until white

2   cups self-rising flour

Icing:

1   16-ounce box confectioners' sugar

½   cup (1 stick) butter

1   teaspoon vanilla extract

    Milk, if needed

Preheat the oven to 300°. Grease and flour 3 9-inch round cake pans. In a large bowl combine the carrots, pecans, sugar, oil, cinnamon, egg whites, and flour. Pour into the prepared pans. Bake for about 30 minutes.

In a medium bowl cream together the confectioners' sugar, butter, and vanilla. Add milk if necessary to make the icing more spreadable. Spread between the layers and on top of the cooled cake.

SERVES 10.

Kenneth Bishop • The Bishops

Nice Orange Slice Cake

1	cup (2 sticks) butter
2	cups sugar
5	eggs
4	cups all-purpose flour
1	teaspoon salt
1	teaspoon soda
1	cup buttermilk
½	pound dates, chopped
1	pound candied orange slices, chopped
1	3½-ounce can flaked coconut
2	cups chopped pecans

Glaze:

½	pound confectioners' sugar
½	cup orange juice
2	teaspoons grated orange rind

Preheat the oven to 250°. Grease a tube pan. In a large bowl cream the butter and sugar. Add the eggs one at a time, beating well after each addition. In a separate bowl sift 3½ cups of the flour, salt, and soda together. Add alternately with the buttermilk to the creamed mixture. Dredge the dates, coconut, nuts, and candy with the remaining flour. Fold into the creamed mixture. Pour into the prepared pan. Bake for 2 hours and 30 minutes.

In a medium bowl combine the confectioners' sugar, orange juice, and orange rind, and mix thoroughly. Pour over the hot cake.

SERVES 10 TO 12.

Naomi Sego Reader • Naomi and the Segos

See the Light Lemonade Cake

1	3-ounce box lemon gelatin
¾	cup hot water
1	18¾-ounce box lemon cake mix
¾	cup oil
4	eggs

Glaze:

1	6-ounce can frozen lemonade concentrate
1	cup sugar

Preheat the oven to 300°. Grease a tube pan. In a large bowl combine the gelatin, hot water, cake mix, oil, and eggs, and beat with an electric mixer for 5 minutes (time this step for the right consistency). Pour the mixture into the prepared pan. Bake for 1 hour. Do not let the cake cool completely before the next step.

In a small bowl mix the lemonade and sugar together with a wooden spoon. (Do not thaw the lemonade.) Pour over the cake while still warm, but not hot.

SERVES 10.

Heather Campbell • Executive Director • SGMA Hall of Fame and Museum

Heavenly Pumpkin Roll

This has become a tradition for our family for any holiday. The children all want the pumpkin roll both before and after dinner!

3	eggs
1	cup sugar
⅔	cup pumpkin
1	teaspoon lemon juice
¾	cup all-purpose flour
2	teaspoons ground cinnamon
1	teaspoon baking powder
½	teaspoon salt
1	teaspoon ground ginger
1	teaspoon grated nutmeg
	Confectioners' sugar

Filling:

1¼	cups confectioners' sugar
1	8-ounce package cream cheese
¼	cup (½ stick) margarine
½	teaspoon vanilla extract

Bluefield, West Virginia, native Joani Tabor can reach four octaves with her voice and also plays the piano, organ, and flute. The motto of the MorningStar Record label artist is "Nothing's gonna steal my joy."

Preheat the oven to 375°. Grease a jelly roll cake pan. In a large bowl beat the eggs with an electric mixer for 5 minutes. Gradually add the sugar. Add the pumpkin and lemon juice. In a separate bowl combine the flour, cinnamon, baking powder, salt, ginger, and nutmeg, and mix together. Add the dry ingredients to the liquid mixture. Pour into the prepared pan. Bake for 15 minutes.

While the cake is still hot, sprinkle confectioners' sugar on a dish towel and roll the cake jelly-roll fashion into the towel while still hot.

In a medium bowl combine the confectioners' sugar, cream cheese, margarine, and vanilla, and beat until smooth. Unroll the cooled cake and ice the inside. Roll the cake back up and garnish with confectioners' sugar or other decoration.

SERVES 10.

Joani Tabor

Because He Lives Red Raspberry Cake and Icing

1	18¾-ounce box white cake mix
3	tablespoons all-purpose flour
1	small package raspberry gelatin
½	cup cold water
1	cup cooking oil
4	eggs
1	10-ounce package frozen red raspberries, halved

Icing:

½	cup (1 stick) butter
1	16-ounce confectioners' sugar

Preheat the oven to 350°. Grease 3 8-inch cake pans. In a large bowl combine the cake mix, flour, and gelatin. Add the water, oil, and eggs, one at a time. Don't overbeat. Break up half of the package of frozen raspberries, and save the other half for the icing. Add the raspberries to the batter. Pour into the prepared pans. Bake at 350° until golden.

In a medium bowl combine the butter, confectioners' sugar, and reserved raspberries, and mix together until spreadable. Spread over the cake.

SERVES 10 TO 12.

Bill and Gloria Gaither

Bill Gaither accepts an award from Jim Myers, left, SESAC's director of international relations, in 1972.

Bill and Gloria Gaither

The husband and wife partnership of Bill and Gloria Gaither is one of the most bountiful in Southern Gospel. They may very well be the contemporary king and queen of the genre for their multiplicity of creative arenas, from singing and songwriting to entrepreneurial success with innumerable books and videos.

Gloria was born in Battle Creek, Michigan, and earned degrees at Anderson University and Ball State University. While substitute teaching in French class at Alexandria High School in Alexandria, Indiana, she met an English teacher, Bill Gaither, and on December 22, 1962, the couple became husband and wife.

Gloria has authored twelve books, including *Let's Hide the World* and *Let's Make a Memory* (co-authored with Shirley Dobson). She has written the lyrics to more than six hundred songs, including such classics as "Because He Lives," "The King Is Coming," "Something About That Name," "Upon this Rock," "I Am a Promise," and "Let's Just Praise the Lord."

She has co-written a dozen musicals and she produced the Homecoming Kids video series for children, The Branch Office. As a singer with The Gaither Trio, Gloria has recorded more than sixty albums and is the lyricist of twenty Dove Award-winning songs.

The mother of three children, as well as a grandmother, Gloria teaches songwriting at Anderson University. About collaboration with her husband, she says, "Bill is a terrific idea person. He comes up with truly original thoughts pulled from everyday life. Delivering those ideas in lyric form is my job. People often ask, 'Which comes first, the music or the words?' The answer is the idea."

As for gospel music, she says, "A lot of people consider music to be distracting or an escape. But gospel music is different. Instead of saying, "give me the next hour and you won't have to think about your problems, gospel music says, Give me the next three minutes and I want you to think more about your life than you've ever thought before."

The most famous gospel music songwriting duo of them all is Bill and Gloria Gaither. Both perform in The Gaither Trio, while Bill headlines The Gaither Vocal Band. The Gaithers have brought more attention to gospel music in recent years with their series of videotapes featuring the greatest names in Southern Gospel.

Bill Gaither wears just about every hat there is in the music business but considers himself first a schoolteacher and coach. Aside from his creative ventures, he is also a preservationist, historian, and trailblazer.

The singer-songwriter of hundreds of tunes, he is a personal friend to all the greats in gospel music and has given a boost to many young singers before they were stars. While a high school teacher, he and his brother and sister would perform weekends harmonizing in churches. By 1963, the Gaither Vocal Band was born and began moving from church assembly halls to high school auditoriums and then larger venues.

During this time his songwriting prowess came to the forefront with "He Touched Me." The song earned Gaither a 1969 Grammy nomination, and was recorded by legions of singers, including Elvis Presley. It also won him the Dove Award as songwriter of the year, and from 1972 to 1977 he continued to reign over that Dove category.

His music went to even greater heights in 1970 after connecting with arranger Ron Huff. And then in 1975, Bill and Gloria formed Praise Gathering for Believers at the Indianapolis Convention Center. The three-day musical and education event now draws more than 10,000 people and has led to other great events like Family Fest and the Jubilate.

His Gaither Vocal Band has featured such artists as Sandy Patti (eight years), Carman (six years), Michael English (ten years), Steve Green (six years), Mark Lowry (nine years), Don Francisco, and Jon Mohr.

Then in the early 1990s, Bill began collecting the history of Southern Gospel in series of twenty videotaped reunions. He gathered the pioneers in one room in a studio in Alexandria and captured them singing the songs that inspired them.

His first tape, *Homecoming,* was such an incredible success that it led to nineteen more videos and sales of more than two million videos with such titles as *Old Friend, Turn Your Radio On, Landmark,* and *Reunion.*

His concept then jumped to television as a one-hour Nashville Network special, *A Gospel Reunion at the Ryman,* in November 1995, and TNN continues to ask for more specials. In 1997, Bill and Gloria Gaither became the first musical artists to be inducted into the Christian Bookseller Association's Hall of Honor.

Says Bill of his success in the field of Christian entertainment, "Christian music is not a style, it's theology wrapped in a lot of different styles; therefore, the artists have become segmented. The videos have been unifying. Gloria and I have always been a bridge. Our circle ranges from presidential candidates to college students. It encompasses all."

The Gaither Vocal Band is composed of (left to right) lead singer Guy Penrod, comedian and baritone Mark Lowry, founder Bill Gaither, and tenor David Phelps.

Ruby Red Cake

I've never been a real big sweet eater. However, my older sister, Ruby, made a cake that has always been my favorite. She called it "Red Velvet Cake," but I renamed it "Ruby Red Cake." Every time she came to visit she would bake one for me. My sister passed away several years ago, and I miss her very much. There will never be another Ruby. She was a very special lady and sister. So, I would like to include this recipe in loving memory of my sister, Ruby Younce-Hamby.

½   cup vegetable shortening

1½   cups sugar

3   eggs

1   ounce red food coloring

2½   cups cake flour

2   heaping teaspoons cocoa

1   teaspoon salt

1   teaspoon baking soda

1   cup buttermilk

1   teaspoon vanilla extract

1   teaspoon vinegar

Icing:

¼   cup all-purpose flour

1½   cups milk

1½   cups sugar

1½   cups (3 sticks) margarine

1½   teaspoon vanilla extract

Grease 3 9-inch round cake pans. Preheat the oven to 350°. In a large bowl blend the shortening, sugar, eggs, and food coloring. In a separate bowl sift together the flour, cocoa, salt, and soda. Add the dry ingredients and buttermilk alternately to the sugar mixture. Stir in the vanilla and vinegar. Pour into the prepared pans. Bake at 350° for 20 to 25 minutes.

   In the top of a double boiler over simmering water cook the flour and milk until thickened, and cool. In a large bowl cream together the sugar, margarine, and vanilla. Add the cooked flour and milk mixture, and beat for 10 minutes. Spread over the cake.

SERVES 10 TO 12.

George Younce • The Cathedrals

The Blue Ridge Quartet was organized in 1946 and by 1964 featured members Elmo Fagg, second tenor and manager; Kenny Gates, baritone and pianist; Edward Sprouse, first tenor; Bill Crow, baritone, and George Younce, bass.

The Cathedrals of 1983 were, clockwise from bottom left, Glen Payne, Mark Trammel, Roger Bennett, Kirk Talley, and George Younce.

There'll Be a Pay Day Red Velvet Cake

½   cup shortening

1½   cups sugar

2   eggs

1   ounce red food coloring

1   ounce water

2   tablespoons cocoa

1   cup buttermilk

2   cups all-purpose flour

1   teaspoon salt

1   teaspoon vanilla extract

1   tablespoon vinegar

1½   teaspoons baking soda

Icing:

1   cup milk

¼   cup all-purpose flour

1   cup sugar

½   cup shortening

½   cup (1 stick) butter

1   teaspoon vanilla extract

Preheat the oven to 350°. Grease 3 9-inch round cake pans. In a large bowl cream the shortening, sugar, and eggs and blend. Add the food coloring and water, and then add the cocoa. Gradually blend in the buttermilk. Gradually add the flour and salt. Add the vanilla and beat until mixed. Combine the vinegar and soda, and then blend into the batter. Pour the batter into the prepared pans. Bake for 30 to 35 minutes.

In a saucepan over medium heat, cook the milk and flour until thick. Let cool. Add the sugar, shortening, and butter. Add the vanilla and beat with an electric mixer on high until fluffy. Ice between each layer and on top.

Hint: For best results use Blue Bonnet whipped margarine or real butter and whole or 2 percent milk.

SERVES 10 TO 12.

Diana Gillette • The Perry Sisters

Keeping the Faith Red Velvet Cake

1	cup (1 stick) butter
2	cups sugar
2	eggs
1	tablespoon vinegar
1	tablespoon cocoa
½	teaspoon salt
1½	teaspoons baking soda
2½	cups cake flour
1	cup buttermilk
1	teaspoon vanilla extract
1	ounce red food coloring

Icing:

1	8-ounce package cream cheese, softened
1	16-ounce box confectioners' sugar
1	teaspoon vanilla extract
	Dash salt

Preheat the oven to 350°. Grease 3 9-inch round cake pans. In a large bowl cream the butter and sugar. Add the eggs and beat until fluffy. Make a paste of vinegar and cocoa and add to the mixture. In a separate bowl sift the salt and baking soda with the flour; add to the mixture, alternating with the buttermilk. Blend well. Add the vanilla and food coloring. Mix well. Pour into the prepared pans and bake for about 30 minutes. Do not bake too long. Some ovens do not take this long. Test the cake by inserting a toothpick in the middle until it comes out clean instead of going by the time.

In a medium bowl combine the cream cheese, confectioners' sugar, vanilla, and salt, and blend until smooth. Spread the icing on the cake.

SERVES 10 TO 12.

Dwayne Burke • Jericho

Queen Ann Cake

This is a favorite recipe of our friends and family.

Charles Johnson is always looking in the right direction with his music.

1   *18¾-ounce box Duncan Hines cake mix (Chocolate Swiss or Devil's Food)*

1   *3½-ounce box instant vanilla pudding*

1   *cup vegetable oil*

3   *eggs*

¼   *cup milk*

Icing:

1   *8-ounce package cream cheese, softened to room temperature*

1   *cup confectioners' sugar*

1   *cup sugar*

5   *plain Hershey's chocolate bars, shaved*

1   *cup nuts, finely chopped (optional)*

1   *12-ounce carton nondairy whipped topping*

Preheat the oven to 325°. Grease 3 8-inch cake pans. In a large bowl sift the cake and pudding mixes together. In a separate bowl beat the oil, eggs, and milk. Add the liquid mixture to the dry ingredients and beat well. Pour the batter the prepared pans. Bake for 30 to 40 minutes or until a toothpick inserted in the center of a cake comes out clean.

In a medium bowl combine the cream cheese, confectioners sugar, and sugar, and beat until very creamy. Fold in the Hershey bar pieces and nuts. Gently fold in the whipped topping. Spread the icing between the layers and over the top and sides of the cake.

SERVES 10.

Annie and Charles Johnson • Charles Johnson & the Revivers

Upside-Down German Chocolate Cake

1	cup shredded coconut
1	cup chopped pecans
1	18¾-ounce box German chocolate cake mix
1	16-ounce box confectioners' sugar
½	cup (1 stick) margarine
1	8-ounce package cream cheese

Preheat the oven to 350°. Sprinkle the coconut and pecans in a 9 x 13 x 2-inch pan. In a large bowl mix the cake mix as directed on the package. Pour the batter over the coconut and pecans. In a large bowl mix the confectioners' sugar, margarine, and cream cheese. Drop by the spoonful on the cake before baking. Bake for 45 minutes or until done.

SERVES 9 TO 12.

Valerie Bell • Homeland Records

Life mates Eddy and Valerie Bell of Paducah, Kentucky, recorded an album in 1990. Eddy played with The Hemphills from 1983 to 1990 and now performs with The Whites every weekend on the Grand Ole Opry as well as on road dates. Valerie has worked in the Southern Gospel music industry since the mid-1980s.

Dewey Like It Turtle Cake

1	18¾-ounce box German chocolate cake mix
¾	cup butter or margarine
1	14-ounce bag caramels
½	cup evaporated milk
1	cup semi-sweet chocolate chips
1	cup chopped pecans

Preheat the oven to 350°. In a large bowl mix the cake as directed on the box. Pour half of the cake batter into a 9 x 13-inch pan. Bake for 15 minutes.

In a medium saucepan melt and mix together the butter, caramels, and milk. Pour the mixture over the cooled cake. Sprinkle with the chocolate chips and nuts. Cover with the remaining batter and bake for 20 minutes more. Sprinkle with more nuts, if desired. Let cool. Serve with whipped topping. Enjoy!

SERVES 8.

Suzanne Young • The Deweys

Grin and Snicker Cake

1	18¾-ounce package German chocolate cake mix
½	cup (1 stick) margarine
⅓	cup milk
1	12-ounce package caramel
1	cup (6 ounces) chocolate chips
1	cup nuts

Preheat the oven to 350°. Grease a 9 x 13-inch pan. In a large bowl prepare the cake mix as directed on the package. Pour half of the batter into the prepared pan. Bake for 20 minutes.

Cool the cake for 10 minutes.

In the top of a double boiler over simmering water melt the margarine, milk, and caramels together. Pour the mixture over the part of the batter that has been baked. Sprinkle with chocolate chips and nuts. Pour the rest of the batter over the nuts. Bake at 250° for 20 minutes, and then at 350° for 10 minutes.

SERVES 10.

Debra Talley • The Talley Trio

Judy's Mississippi Mud Cake

1   cup shortening

2   cups sugar

4   eggs

1½   cups all-purpose flour

⅓   cup cocoa

1   teaspoon vanilla extract

¼   teaspoon salt

1   cup chopped pecans

1   10½-ounce package miniature marshmallows

Frosting:

1   cup (2 sticks) margarine

1   16-ounce package confectioners' sugar

½   cup cocoa

3   teaspoons vanilla extract

Preheat the oven to 325°. In a large bowl cream the shortening and sugar. Add the eggs and vanilla, and mix together. Add the dry ingredients and nuts. Mix well. Pout into an 8-inch square baking pan. Bake for 25 minutes. Top immediately with marshmallows and cool for 5 minutes. Frost immediately.

   In a medium bowl combine the margarine, confectioners' sugar, cocoa, and vanilla, and mix well. Oour over the top of the marshmallows. Spread. Refrigerate overnight before cutting. It's very rich.

SERVES 6 TO 8.

Judy Spencer • Manna Music

Amber's Chocolate Layer Cake

Every year we try to have a unique birthday cake for our daughter, Amber, but it seems we always keep coming to a chocolate layer cake. It's Amber's favorite, and this is her favorite recipe. —Jerry and Kelly Nelon Thompson

½   cup shortening or butter

1½   cups sugar

3   eggs, separated

2   1-ounce squares bitter chocolate,
       melted

1   teaspoon baking soda

1¼   cups buttermilk

2   cups sifted cake flour

¼   teaspoon salt

1   teaspoon vanilla extract

Icing (uncooked):

1   cup shortening

¼   teaspoon salt

2   egg yolks

3   1-ounce squares bitter chocolate,
       melted

2   cups confectioners' sugar

3   tablespoons cream

Grandfather Rex Nelon shows off his youngest grand-daughter, Autumn Lyn Thompson, as big sister Amber and parents Kelly and Jerry Thompson share their joy.

Preheat the oven to 350°. Grease 3 8-inch or 2 9-inch round pans. In a large bowl cream the shortening and then add the sugar, egg yolks, and melted chocolate. Mix the soda in the buttermilk and add alternately with the flour to the creamed mixture. In a separate bowl combine the salt and egg whites and beat until stiff. Fold into the mixture. Add the vanilla. Pour into the prepared pans. Bake for 20 minutes.

   In a medium bowl blend the shortening with the salt, egg yolks, and chocolate. Add the sugar and cream, and beat well. Spread between the layers and on the top and sides of the cake.

SERVES 10 TO 12.

Amber Thompson • The Nelons

Tasty Chocolate Torte Cake

1   18¾-ounce package yellow cake mix

2   eggs, slightly beaten

2½   tablespoons (⅓ stick) soft margarine

Filling:

1   package chocolate fudge frosting mix

2   cups whipping cream

1   teaspoon vanilla extract

1   cup nuts

Preheat the oven to 350°. In a large bowl combine the cake mix, margarine, and eggs thoroughly with a fork or pastry blender. Shape the dough into 6 equal parts. With a well-floured rolling pin, roll each part onto the bottom of an inverted 9-inch round cake pan. Bake for 8 to 10 minutes or until the edges are brown. While warm, carefully loosen with a thin knife and ease onto a clean cloth to cool.

In a mixing bowl combine the frosting mix, whipping cream, vanilla, and nuts, and mix well. Chill thoroughly.

Beat the filling mixture with an electric mixer until stiff. Spread the filling between each layer of cake. Allow the cake to mellow in the refrigerator overnight in a cake taker.

SERVES 10.

The Brashear Family

The Rex Nelon Singers, performing for Gospel Country in 1984, was then composed of, left to right, Rodney Swain, Karen Peck, Jerry Thompson, Kelly Nelon Thompson, and Rex Nelon.

Cheerful Chocolate-Covered Cherry Cake

1   18¾-ounce box Pillsbury Plus Devil's Food Cake Mix

2   eggs

1   teaspoon almond extract

1   21-ounce can cherry pie filling

Icing:

1   cup sugar

5   tablespoons butter

⅓   cup milk

1   12-ounce package chocolate chips

Preheat the oven to 325°. In a large bowl combine the cake mix, eggs, almond extract, and cherry pie filling, and mix with a spoon until blended. Spread the batter in a 9 x 13-inch baking pan. Bake for 30 to 40 minutes.

In a saucepan combine the sugar, butter, and milk. Boil for 1 minute. Remove the pan from the heat and mix in the chocolate chips until melted. Spread over the cake.

SERVES 9 TO 12.

Peg McKamey Bean and Ruben Bean • The McKameys

The McKameys perform at the 1997 Hearts Aflame Awards show.

Little Jan's Dump Cake

1	14-ounce can crushed pineapple
1	21-ounce can cherry pie filling
1	18¾-ounce box super moist butter recipe cake mix
1	cup (2 sticks) butter

Preheat the oven to 325°. Dump the pineapple in a 9 x 13-inch pan and spread evenly. Dump the cherry pie filling on top of the pineapples and spread evenly without mixing with the pineapples. Dump the cake mix into the pan and spread evenly, again without mixing with the other ingredients. Cut the butter into pats and cover the top of the cake. Bake for 45 minutes.

This is good with anything—ice cream, whipped topping, peanut butter, you name it. You know me—Ms. Patience. Dump-spread, dump-spread, dump-spread. That's what I like—quick and eat!

SERVES 8.

Little Jan Buckner

Little Jan, as she is affectionately known, has spent her adult life as half of the Sunliters, Wendy Bagwell's singing partners. The group enjoyed many firsts in Southern Gospel music, including being the first group to play Carnegie Hall and the first group to sell a million copies of a song ("Here Come the Rattlesnakes"). Since Wendy's death in 1996, Little Jan is continuing her love of gospel music by traveling and singing as a solo artist.

I'm So Excited Italian Cream Cake

½   cup (1 stick) butter

¾   cup vegetable oil

2   cups sugar

5   eggs, separated

1   cup buttermilk

1   teaspoon baking soda

2   cups all-purpose flour, sifted

1   teaspoon vanilla extract

1   cup shredded coconut

1   cup chopped pecans

Icing:

1   8-ounce package cream cheese, softened

½   cup (1 stick) butter, softened

1   teaspoon vanilla extract

1   16-ounce box confectioners' sugar

1   cup finely chopped nuts

1   cup shredded coconut (optional)

Preheat the oven to 325°. Grease and flour a 9 x 13-inch cake pan for a sheet cake or 3 8-or 9-inch layer pans. In a large bowl cream the butter, oil, and sugar. Add the egg yolks one at a time, beating after each addition. Stir the baking soda into the buttermilk. Add the sifted flour to the batter alternately with the buttermilk mixture. Add the vanilla, coconut, and pecans. In a medium bowl beat the egg whites into stiff peaks and fold into the mixture. Pour into the prepared pans. Bake for 45 minutes or until done. Cool and ice.

  In a medium bowl beat the cream cheese and butter until blended. Add the vanilla, confectioners' sugar, nuts, and coconut, and continue to beat until the icing is spreadable.

SERVES 10.

Candy Hemphill-Christmas

World's Greasiest Cheesecake

Crust:

1   12-ounce box vanilla wafers, crushed fine

½   cup (1 stick) and 1 tablespoon butter, melted

1   cup chopped pecans

Pie:

3   8-ounce packages cream cheese, softened

1½   cups sugar

4   eggs

1   pint sour cream

1   cup sugar

In a medium bowl mix the vanilla wafers, butter, and pecans, and press into a 10-inch spring-form pan.

Preheat the oven to 325°. In a mixing bowl combine the cream cheese and the 1½ cups of sugar and beat until creamy. Add the eggs one at a time, beating after each addition. When the mixture is well blended, pour it into the vanilla wafer crust. Place the pan in the center of the preheated oven and bake for 45 to 50 minutes.

In a medium bowl combine the sour cream and the 1 cup of sugar. When the cheesecake is leathery and no longer wet looking (after 45 to 50 minutes), pour the sour cream mixture over the cake and bake for an additional 10 minutes. Cool completely, then place in the refrigerator overnight.

This cake can be frozen for several months before serving.

SERVES 8.

Daywind Music Group

Members of Daywind Music Group pose in their "Everybody Loves a Winner" jerseys while at the 1996 National Quartet Convention.

Very Strawberry Cheesecake

3	tablespoons melted butter
1	tablespoon sugar
1½	cups graham cracker crumbs
2	tablespoons softened butter
1½	8-ounce packages (12 ounces) cream cheese, softened
½	cup sugar
2	eggs
2	tablespoons all-purpose flour
⅔	cup light cream
½	cup lemon juice
2	teaspoons grated lemon rind
2	cups sour cream
2	pints whole strawberries
½	cup strawberry jelly, melted

Preheat the oven to 325°. In a medium bowl combine the melted butter, 1 tablespoon of sugar, and graham cracker crumbs, and mix well. Press into the bottom of an 8-inch pie pan.

In a large bowl cream the 2 tablespoons butter, cream cheese, and ½ cup of sugar until light and fluffy. Add the eggs one at a time, beating well after each addition. Add the flour, cream, lemon juice, and rind, and mix well. Pour into the crumb crust. Bake for 35 minutes. Spread the sour cream over the top. Bake for 5 minutes longer. Dip the strawberries in the jelly and arrange on the cooled cheesecake. Chill for about 4 hours.

SERVES 6 TO 8.

Mike Holcomb • The Inspirations

Martha's Quick and Easy No-Bake Strawberry Cheesecake

1	14-ounce can sweetened condensed milk
1	8-ounce package cream cheese, softened
¼	cup lemon juice
1	teaspoon vanilla extract
1	store-bought 9-inch graham cracker pie shell
	Graham cracker crumbs

Topping:

1	pint strawberries (fresh, if available)
	Strawberry glaze

In a large bowl beat the sweetened condensed milk, cream cheese, lemon juice, and vanilla with an electric beater until thickened. Pour into the pie shell. Sprinkle with graham cracker crumbs. Cover with the plastic top from the pie shell and refrigerate for a few hours or overnight.

Mix the strawberries and the glaze. Spread evenly over the cheesecake. Refrigerate until ready to serve. It keeps for 3 or 4 days in the refrigerator.

SERVES 6 TO 8.

Martha Carson

Medlocks Millionaire Pie

1   14-ounce can sweetened condensed milk

1   20-ounce can crushed pineapple, well-drained

2   tablespoons lemon juice

1   cup chopped pecans

1   8-ounce carton nondairy whipped topping

2   9-inch graham cracker crusts

In a large bowl mix together the sweetened condensed milk, pineapple, and lemon juice. Fold in the pecans and whipped topping. Pour into the graham cracker crusts and refrigerate.

MAKES 2 PIES, OR 12 TO 16 SERVINGS.

Tina Medlock • The Medlocks

The Medlocks are a family quartet of two brothers who married two sisters. Rickey and Rhonda began their ministry the year they were married, 1976. A few years later they were joined by Steven and Tina Medlock.

Here Comes the Fudge Pie

¼   cup (½ stick) margarine

1½   cups sugar

3   tablespoons cocoa

½   cup evaporated milk

2   eggs

1   teaspoon vanilla extract

1   8-inch unbaked pie shell

Preheat the oven to 400°. In a heavy saucepan melt the margarine. Turn off the heat. Add the sugar and cocoa. In a medium bowl mix the evaporated milk, eggs, and vanilla. Add the cocoa mixture, and mix well. Pour into an unbaked pie shell and bake at 400° for 10 minutes. Reduce heat to 350° and bake for 25 minutes more.

SERVES 6 TO 8.

Susan Nimmo • Harper & Associates

Susan Nimmo takes to the dance floor with son David at his wedding reception in December 1997.

Fudge Pie Blackwood

½   cup (1 stick) margarine

¾   cup all-purpose flour

1   cup sugar

2   eggs, beaten

1   teaspoon vanilla extract

¼   cup cocoa

¾   cup chopped nuts (optional)

Preheat the oven to 325° In a small saucepan melt the margarine. In a large bowl mix together the flour and sugar, then add the melted margarine and stir. Add the beaten eggs and stir. Add the vanilla and stir. Stir in the cocoa and nuts. Pour into an 8-inch pie pan. Bake for 25 to 30 minutes, depending on your oven and how done you want it. It's best when not overcooked.

It's very good when served hot with ice cream.

SERVES 6 TO 8.

James Blackwood

The Blackwood Brothers in this vintage photograph are, left to right, Bill Shaw, Whitey Gleason, James Blackwood, John Hall, and Cecil Blackwood.

The Blackwood Brothers, left to right, piano player Dave Wesson, James Blackwood, Bill Shaw, Cecil Blackwood, and John Hall, harmonized on The Porter Wagoner Show, *(that's Porter at far right), in the 1960s.*

The Blackwood Brothers in their early days.

The Blackwood Brothers

The Blackwood Brothers came out of the Mississippi delta country in 1934 to be one of the biggest groups in Southern Gospel history. The original quartet was comprised of brothers Roy (first tenor), Doyle (bass and playing guitar), and James Blackwood (lead), and Roy's son R.W. (baritone).

When the quartet wandered over to WHEF Radio in Kosciusko, Mississippi, and performed one Sunday, the phone rang off the hook with calls from listeners thrilled by their close, pleasing harmonies. That success led to touring the state—playing dates and peddling Vaughan Music Company songbooks. In 1939 they became The Blackwood Brothers Stamps Quartet as they sold songbooks for the Stamps company.

After a sixteen-month stint in Shreveport, Louisiana., V.O. Stamps got The Blackwoods to replace The Stamps Quartet in Iowa, and in 1940 the brothers began playing a 5,000-watt station in Shenandoah, Iowa. Before World War II, The Blackwoods were wooing a radio audience of more than one million listeners.

After a halt because of the world war, The Blackwoods reunited in the late 1940s and became so popular that they split into two groups, and by 1950, when they moved back South from Iowa, they were the most popular gospel singing group in the country. In 1951 they became the first gospel group to ever record an album when they went into the studio for RCA Victor.

Into the 1950s, The Blackwoods and The Statesmen held the Southern Gospel world in the palm of their hands with their great musical duels, but tragedy struck in the summer of 1954, when, just after winning *Arthur Godfrey's Talent Scouts* show, a plane crash took the lives of R.W. Blackwood and bass singer Bill Lyles.

James Blackwood was ready to give up the concert trail but decided to keep the faith, so he got R.W.'s brother Cecil to fill the baritone slot and Lyle's bass position was covered by J.D. Sumner, who moved over from The Sunshine Boys.

With Sumner aboard The Blackwoods rebounded and regained their place in popularity.

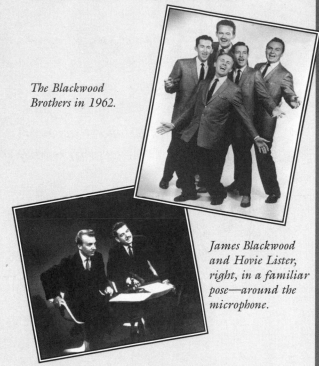

The Blackwood Brothers in 1962.

James Blackwood and Hovie Lister, right, in a familiar pose—around the microphone.

But Sumner brought along several touches of his own. The Blackwood Brothers became the first Southern gospel quartet to travel by bus after Sumner built them a customized bus in 1955, transforming a 1937 Aerocoach from Trailways into a rolling bunkhouse.

The Blackwoods of the 1990s are James Blackwood, Cecil Blackwood, Jimmy Blackwood, Pat Hoffmaster, Ken Turner, and Tommy Fairchild. The group has sold more than fifteen million records and won dozens of gospel music awards, including Grammys and Doves.

James Blackwood, known as "Mr. Gospel Music," holds the record for receiving the Gospel Music Association male vocalist of the year award the most times with seven Doves to his credit. Cecil Stamps Blackwood, who, as a teenager, organized The Songfellows (whose members included future Kingsmen Quartet member Jimmy Hammil and future rock 'n' roll king Elvis Presley), is director of the Blackwood Brothers Evangelistic Association, which he founded in the 1970s.

Pleasing Peanut Butter Pie

Crust:

1¼   cups chocolate cookie crumbs

¼   cup sugar

¼   cup melted butter or margarine

Filling:

1   8-ounce package cream cheese, softened

1   cup creamy peanut butter (or crunchy, if preferred)

1   cup sugar

1   teaspoon vanilla extract

1   cup whipping cream, whipped

In a medium bowl combine the crust ingredients, and press into a 9-inch pie pan. Bake at 350° for 10 to 12 minutes.

In a large bowl beat the cream cheese, peanut butter, sugar, and vanilla until smooth. Fold in the whipped cream. Spoon the filling into the crust. If desired, garnish with shaved chocolate, cookie crumbs, or finely chopped nuts. Refrigerate before serving.

SERVES 6 TO 8.

Fay Shedd • Artist Direction Agency

Let's Talk Peanut Butter Pie

1	3-ounce package cream cheese
1	cup confectioners' sugar
3	tablespoons milk
½	cup peanut butter (crunchy or smooth; I prefer crunchy)
1	8-ounce carton nondairy whipped topping
1	teaspoon vanilla extract
1	9-inch chocolate wafer crust

Mix all of the ingredients together until smooth. Pour into the crust and chill until firm.

You can garnish with crushed peanuts or grated chocolate, or chunks of Reese's Peanut Butter Cups.

SERVES 6 TO 8.

Ann Downing

Ann Downing is one of the few female soloists in Southern Gospel music to have a Top Ten single. She has recorded more than forty albums in three decades of singing. She and her late husband, Paul Downing, were the heart of one of the most popular groups of the 1970s, The Downings.

Perfect Pecan Pie

4	eggs
2	tablespoons all-purpose flour
	Pinch salt
1½	cups sugar
2	tablespoons butter
1½	cups white corn syrup
1	teaspoon vanilla extract
2	cups chopped pecans
2	unbaked 9-inch pie shells

Preheat the oven to 350°. In a large bowl mix the eggs, flour, salt, sugar, butter, corn syrup, vanilla, and pecans. Pour the filling into the unbaked pie shells. Bake for 45 minutes.

MAKES 2 PIES.

Elaine Wilburn • The Wilburns

The Wilburns have shared their gospel talents for over twenty-five years and are known for their standards "God's Promised Land," "Outside the Gate," and "The Hand of the Lord." Clockwise from bottom left are Jackie Wilburn, Loren Harris, Ricky Atkinson, and Elaine Wilburn.

Gold City Caramel Pie

2   9-inch deep-dish pie crusts, baked and cooled

½   cup (1 stick) butter

7   ounces flaked coconut

1½   cups chopped pecans, toasted in microwave for 2 to 3 minutes

1   8-ounce package cream cheese, softened

1   14-ounce can sweetened condensed milk

1   16-ounce carton nondairy whipped topping

1   16-ounce jar caramel ice cream topping, thinned in microwave

In a saucepan melt the butter and mix with the coconut and pecans. Set aside. In a separate bowl mix the cream cheese, sweetened condensed milk, and whipped topping. Put a layer of the cream cheese mixture in the bottom of each pie crust and then a layer of the pecan mixture. Next drizzle with caramel. Repeat with another layer of each. Freeze overnight before serving. Keep in the freezer.

MAKES 2 PIES.

Tim Riley • Gold City Quartet

Gold City struck pay dirt with major hits from 1982 to 1990 in "Midnight Cry," "Getting Ready To Leave This World," "When I Get Carried Away," and "I Think I'll Read It Again." They were four-time group of the year from The Singing News *Fan Awards. Left to right are Jay Parrack, Jonathan Wilburn, Mark Trammell, and Tim Riley.*

Treasures Pecan Chess Pie

This recipe is one that is passed down from my aunt. When I was a little girl, my dad's family always had a big Christmas get-together. And I would always ask my Aunt Margaret to make my favorite pecan pie. Since I have been married, this is always a request from my father-in-law at Thanksgiving and Christmas. I hope you enjoy it as much as my family does.

1	*cup firmly packed light brown sugar*
1	*tablespoon all-purpose flour*
1	*tablespoon milk*
½	*cup margarine, melted*
½	*cup sugar*
2	*eggs*
1	*teaspoon vanilla*
1	*cup chopped pecans*
1	*unbaked 9-inch pie shell*

Preheat the oven to 325°. In a large bowl combine the brown sugar, flour, milk, margarine, sugar, eggs, vanilla, and pecans. Mix together and pour into the pie shell. Bake for 45 minutes.

SERVES 6 TO 8.

Amy Lambert-Templeton

Amy Lambert-Templeton busy in her kitchen.

Great Pumpkin Pie

1   cup firmly packed brown sugar

2   tablespoons all-purpose flour

½   teaspoon salt

¼   teaspoon ground cinnamon

¼   teaspoon grated nutmeg

1   cup cooked pumpkin (canned)

2   cups evaporated milk

2   eggs, beaten

1   unbaked 9-inch pie shell

     Whipped topping

Preheat the oven to 450°. In a medium bowl mix the sugar, flour, salt, and spices together. In a large bowl combine the pumpkin and the dry ingredients. Add the milk and eggs. Pour the filling into the pie shell. Bake for 10 minutes.

Reduce the heat to 350° and continue baking for another 25 to 30 minutes or until the filling is firm and a knife inserted in the pie comes out clean.

Garnish with whipped topping when completely cool. Have fun eating!

SERVES 6 TO 8.

Ronnie Hutchins • The Inspirations

Ethel's Sweet Potato Pie

3	sweet potatoes (or enough for 2 cups), boiled and peeled
¼	cup (½ stick) butter
2	eggs
1	cup sugar
½	cup whole milk
½	teaspoon ground nutmeg
5	drops vanilla extract
	Dash salt
1	unbaked 9-inch pie shell

Preheat the oven to 350°. In a mixing bowl cream together the sweet potatoes, butter, and eggs. Add the sugar and mix together. Add the milk, nutmeg, vanilla, and salt, and mix thoroughly. Pour the filling into the pie shell. Bake for 35 to 40 minutes.

SERVES 6 TO 8.

The Fairfield Four

Members of the famed Fairfield Four during the late 1990s are (left to right) lead singers Joe Rice and Robert Hamlett, tenor Wilson Waters, Jr., baritone James Hill, and bass singer Isaac Freeman.

The Fairfield Four

Called "a national musical treasure," the Fairfield Four was founded as a trio in 1921 at Nashville's Fairfield Baptist Church. After winning a singing contest for which part of the prize package was a chance to sing on 50,000-watt WLAC Radio, the a capella masters began to build a national following. The group even had its own radio show five days a week from the early '40s to early '50s. (Current Fairfield Four baritone James Hill was all of thirty years old when he joined the group in 1946.)

The group began to receive calls to appear all over the country, and soon they were beginning their first formal tours. As with any group whose history spans most of a century, there were changes of personnel through the years. (Even James Hill and Isaac Freeman left to form the Skylarks in 1950.) And from 1960 to 1980, not much was heard from the Fairfield Four outside of occasional performances fairly close to Nashville.

In October 1980, a quartet reunion show in Birmingham provided an opportunity for members of the Fairfield Four to reunite. There that day were James Hill, Isaac Freeman, the Rev. Sam McCrary, Willie Love, and guitarist Joe Whittaker. Inspired by the warm reception to their reunited sound, the group began to perform regularly again. They've been red-hot ever since. Key members in the group since the reunion have included Walter Settles and W.L. Richardson. Today's Fairfield Four consists of James Hill, Isaac Freeman, Wilson Waters, Jr., Robert Hamlett, and Joe Rice.

With an enthusiasm and extraordinary sound that are just as effective and contagious when performed in either small-town churches or in Carnegie Hall, the National Heritage Fellowship winners are among the greatest emissaries of gospel harmony ever to use their voices to sing songs of praise.

Though the Fairfield Four is in demand for harmonizing in the studio and on stage with the likes of Elvis Costello, Lyle Lovett, Steve Earle, and the Nashville Bluegrass Band, their roots remain firmly planted in the gospel music tradition. Their 1997 Warner Bros. album *I Couldn't Hear Nobody Pray* has won praise from all corners (incuding a Grammy), as did their 1992 release, *Standing in the Safety Zone*.

And one thing's for sure: Nobody in any form of musical entertainment can make a trademark wardrobe of overalls blend with tuxedo jackets and bow ties as well as the Fairfield Four. But that's all part of knowing how to create harmony.

Something Better than Gold Pie

1	14-ounce can sweetened condensed milk
¼	cup pecans
¼	cup pineapple, crushed
¼	cup cherries
½	cup lemon juice
1	9-inch graham cracker pie shell
	Nondairy whipped topping

In a large bowl combine the sweetened condensed milk, pecans, pineapple, cherries, and lemon juice. Pour into the pie shell. Chill for 2 hours.

Top with nondairy whipped topping. Wait another 2 hours before cutting.

SERVES 6 TO 8.

Angelina McKeithen • The McKeithens

Stellar Coconut-Pineapple Pie

3	eggs
½	cup (1 stick) butter, melted
1	8-ounce can crushed pineapple, drained
1½	cups sugar
2½	cups flaked coconut
1	teaspoon vanilla extract
2	9-inch deep dish pie crusts

Vestal Goodman captivates the audience during a Southern Gospel concert at the Ryman Auditorium.

Preheat the oven to 350°. In a large bowl mix the eggs, butter, pineapple, sugar, coconut, and vanilla together. Pour the filling into the crusts. Bake for 30 to 45 minutes. Make sure the pies are a golden brown before removing from oven.

MAKES 2 PIES.

Stella Goodman Messer • The Happy Goodmans

City of Gold Pineapple Pie

1	16-ounce carton nondairy whipped topping
1	8-ounce carton sour cream
1	14-ounce can sweetened condensed milk
1	15-ounce can crushed pineapple, drained
1	cup chopped pecans
6	tablespoons lemon juice
1	9-inch graham cracker pie shells

In a large bowl mix the whipped topping, sour cream, and sweetened condensed milk until smooth. Add the pineapple, nuts, and lemon juice. Pour into 2 pie shells and chill. Keeps for up to 6 weeks in the freezer.

MAKES 2 PIES.

Jonathan Wilburn • Gold City Quartet

Jonathan Wilburn and family.

Japanese Fruit Pie

Next to turkey and dressing, this uncommonly good Japanese fruit pie has become the most common food consumed at the Hinsons' home during the holidays. The fruit pie was introduced to the original Hinsons by a fan while on the road. The group was so impressed with the pie that they immediately got her to write down the recipe. It became a family favorite in no time. However, the hand-written recipe lacked a name, so the tasty dish was affectionately referred to as "that pie." Two years later the group ran into the lady again and allowed her to solve the mystery of the nameless pie.

1   *cup sugar*

½   *cup (1 stick) margarine, melted*

      Pinch salt

2   *eggs, beaten*

1   *tablespoon vinegar*

½   *cup flaked coconut*

½   *cup chopped walnuts*

½   *cup raisins*

1   *9-inch unbaked pie shell*

Preheat the oven to 325°. In a large bowl mix the sugar, margarine, salt, eggs, vinegar, coconut, walnuts, and raisins. Pour the filling into the pie shell. Bake about 25 to 30 minutes until the shell browns. Top with nondairy whipped topping and serve.

Note: For lower cholesterol, use ½ cup of Promise margarine and 2 Egg Beaters instead of regular margarine and eggs.

SERVES 6 TO 8.

The New Hinsons

The New Hinsons of Hendersonville, Tennessee, are headed up by spouses Bo (son of Roy Hinson) and Rhonda Hinson. They captured nominations from the Singing News *Fan Awards for song of the year and single of the year in 1997 for their Number One song "Oasis." Left to right are Bo Hinson, Tim Goude, Stan Daily, Rhonda Hinson, and Terry Hagan.*

Oaks Fresh Berry Pie

¾   cup sugar

3   tablespoons cornstarch

1½   cups water

1   4-ounce package gelatin (any red flavor)

1   cup blueberries

1   cup raspberries

1   cup sliced strawberries

1   9-inch reduced fat graham cracker pie crust

2   cups light nondairy whipped topping, thawed

In a medium saucepan mix the sugar and cornstarch, gradually stirring in the water until smooth. Cook on medium until the mixture come to a boil, stirring constantly. Boil for 1 minute and remove from heat. Stir in the gelatin until completely dissolved. Cool to room temperature and then stir in the berries. Pour the filling into the crust. Refrigerate for 3 hours or until firm.

Garnish with whipped topping and a few berries for decoration.

Variation: Nora Lee likes to add ½ cup chopped pecans to the gelatin mixture or the whipped topping.

SEVES 6 TO 8.

Nora Lee and Duane Allen • The Oak Ridge Boys

Today's country hit group The Oak Ridge Boys can trace its roots back to 1945 in Oak Ridge, Tennessee, where the atomic bomb was being developed. Originally known as The Oak Ridge Quartet, they began performing on the Grand Ole Opry in the fall of '45 and by the mid-1950s were featured in Time *magazine as one of the top-drawing gospel groups in the nation. The "quartet" in 1957 featured, front left to right, Hobart Evans, Ron Page, and Herman Harper, and back left to right, Smitty Gatlin and accompanist Powell Hassell.*

During the late 1960s and early '70s The Oak Ridge Boys were one of the most innovative acts in gospel with their rock approach, a full band, bell-bottom pants, and long hair. The 1971 edition of the group included, front left to right, Mark Ellerbee, Tommy Fairchild, and Don Breland, and, back left to right, Willie Wynn, Duane Allen, Noel Fox, and William Lee Golden.

The Southern Gospel Music Hall of Fame and Museum

A dream that began more than thirty years ago is nearing reality. Ideas and blueprints are currently being transformed into steel and concrete as the Southern Gospel Music Hall of Fame and Museum goes up in Sevierville, Tennessee.

It was during the 1994 National Quartet Convention that the Southern Gospel Music Association (SGMA), the brainchild of *Singing News* publisher Maurice Templeton, came into being. With J.D. Sumner at the helm, the organization sent the forces into motion to select a site and lay the groundwork for the construction of a museum and hall of fame to honor the greats of Southern Gospel.

Sevierville won out because of its popularity as a family tourist destination, its close proximity to Pigeon Forge, Gatlinburg, Dollywood, and the Great Smoky Mountains National Park, and the abundance of hotels, restaurants, shopping venues and performance-style theaters near the Hall of Fame site.

Tennessee state officials estimate that between eight and ten million cars will pass in front of the Southern Gospel Music Hall of Fame and Museum annually.

The Southern Gospel Music Association held its first annual Hall of Fame induction banquet on May 21, 1997, at the Grand Hotel and Convention Center in Pigeon Forge, with about one thousand Southern Gospel music industry people and fans in attendance.

This marked the first formal event in recent history for the Southern Gospel music industry. Among the performers were Greater Vision, The Kingdom Heirs, The Kingsmen, Palmette State Quartet, The Hoppers, and J.D. Sumner and the Stamps, while a special Hall of Fame "quartet" of James Blackwood, Jack Toney, Glen Payne, J.D. Sumner, and Hovie Lister also sang.

W.L. "Wendy" Bagwell was the 1997 inductee and the first person inducted into the SGMA Hall of Fame by the SGMA membership.

The SGMA board also inducted twenty-four individuals into the SGMA Hall of Fame "Deceased" category and thirteen persons into the "Living" category. These had been previously inducted into the Gospel Music Association Hall of Fame.

Inductees into the SGMA Hall of Fame in the "Deceased" category were: Lee Roy Abernathy, W.L. "Wendy" Bagwell, Clarice "Ma" Baxter, J.R. Baxter, Jr., Albert E. Brumley, D.P. "Dad" Carter, Fanny Crosby, Denver Crumpler, John Daniel, Wally Fowler, Rusty Goodman, Connor B. Hall, Herman Harper, Alphus LeFevre, Urias LeFevre, Lowell Mason, B.B. McKinney, Marvin Norcross, W.B. Nowlin, Lloyd Orrell, O.A. Parris, William Morgan Ramsey, G.T. "Dad" Speer, Lena Brock Speer, Frank Stamps, V.O. Stamps, Kieffer G. Vaughan, James D. Vaughan, Jim "Pappy" Waites, W.B. Walbert, James "Big Chief" Wetherington, and R.E. Winsett.

Inductees in the "Living" category were: Les Beasley, James Blackwood, Governor Jimmie Davis, Bill Gaither, Jake Hess, Eva Mae LeFevre, Hovie Lister, Mosie Lister, Glen Payne, Dottie Rambo, Brock Speer, J.D. Sumner, and J.G. Whitfield.

Beginning in May of 1998, the Hall of Fame returns to its standard procedure of adding two new inductees a year.

Those making up the board as of the fall of 1997 include J.D. Sumner, president; Maurice Templeton, vice president; Eddie Crook, secretary; Jim Cumbee, treasurer; Charlie Burke, Russ Farrar, Eldridge Fox, Bill Gaither, Jerry Goff, Tony Greene, Jerry Kirksey, Jack Pittman, and Jack Wolfe.

Fans of Southern Gospel Music may enlist in the two-million dollar fund-raising efforts for the Hall of Fame and Museum. Engraved bricks may be purchased in their name or the name of a loved one as a memorial for one hundred dollars each.

The bricks will go into the Walk of Fame as a permanent part of the Hall of Fame and museum.

Groundbreaking for the Gospel Music Association Hall of Fame and Museum is set for summer 1998 with a grand opening in spring 1999.

Blueberry Surprise

2	3-ounce packages cream cheese
1/2	cup confectioners' sugar
1	3-ounce package Dream Whip
1	angel food cake
2	20-ounce cans blueberry pie filling, chilled

In a mixing bowl combine the cream cheese and confectioners' sugar and mix until it is of smooth consistency. In a separate bowl prepare the Dream Whip according to the package instructions. Add the Dream Whip to the cream cheese mixture and mix together. Break the angel food cake into small pieces and fold them into the mixture. Spread into a 9 x 13-inch pan. Chill.

Spread the chilled blueberry pie filling over the mixture and chill until served.

SERVES 9 TO 12.

The Brashear Family

Weidmann's Black Bottom Pie

"You can find me at lunch on Thursdays eating this pie at Weidemann's Restaurant in downtown Meridian, Mississippi, says Jacky Jack White. "They've been making black bottom pie there since 1870." Jacky Jack features "Black Bottom Pie" in his song "Miss Meridian" on his *Southern Songbook* album with the Carter Sisters.

Crust:

14   *ginger snaps*

5   *tablespoons melted butter*

Custard filling mixture:

2   *cups scalded milk*

4   *egg yolks, well beaten*
      (reserve the whites)

½   *cup sugar*

1½   *tablespoons cornstarch*

1½   *squares bitter chocolate*

1   *teaspoon vanilla extract*

Second Mixture:

1   *tablespoon gelatin*

2   *tablespoons cold water*

4   *egg whites (reserved)*

½   *cup sugar*

¼   *teaspoon cream of tar-*
      tar

2   *tablespoons whiskey*
      extract

Topping:

      Whipped Cream

      Shavings of bitter chocolate

Daywind's Buffalo Run recording artist Jacky Jack White (that's him in the back with the baseball cap) spearheaded the First Annual Southern Gospel Music Songwriters Night at the Bluebird in Nashville, Tennessee. He penned the title cut of the When Men Pray *project, commemorating Fortieth Anniversary of the National Quartet Convention. Among the songwriter participants were Niles Borop, Judy Spencer, Jeff Person, Daryl Williams, Norman Holland, Marty Funderburg, Mervin Loque, Jennifer O'Neill, Lulu Roman, Ken Beck, and Brenda McClain.*

Preheat the oven to 350°. Crush the ginger snaps, roll out fine, add the melted butter, and pat into a 9-inch pan. Bake for 10 minutes and allow to cool.

In the top of a double boiler add the eggs slowly to the hot milk. Stir in the sugar and cornstarch. Cook over simmering water for 20 minutes, stirring occasionally, until the mixture coats the spoon.

Remove 1 cup of the custard to a bowl and add the chocolate. Beat the chocolate mixture well as it cools. Add the vanilla extract, and then pour the chocolate mixture into bottom of the pie crust. Chill.

Dissolve the gelatin in the cold water, then add the custard filling mixture, and let cool.

In a medium bowl beat the egg whites, sugar, cream of tartar, and whiskey extract. Fold into the custard mixture and pour on top of the chocolate mixture. Chill. Before serving, cover the top of the pie with whipped cream, and top with shavings of bitter chocolate.

SERVES 6 TO 8.

Jacky Jack White

Right Out of Redbook Easter Hunt Pie

1	8-ounce package cream cheese, softened
1	14-ounce can sweetened condensed milk
¾	cup cold water
1	3½-ounce package instant vanilla pudding and pie filling
1½	cups nondairy whipped topping, thawed
16	miniature chocolate eggs
1	6-ounce graham cracker pie crust

In a large mixing bowl beat the cheese until fluffy. Gradually beat in the sweetened condensed milk until smooth. Add the water and pudding mix, and beat on low speed until smooth. Gently stir in the whipped topping. Spoon half of the filling into the pie crust. Place the chocolate eggs evenly over the filling. Top with the remaining filling. Chill for 3 hours. Garnish as desired.

SERVES 6 TO 8.

Kathy Williams • Homeland Records

I Declare Chocolate Eclair Cake

1   *16-ounce package graham crackers, crumbled*

2   *8-ounce packages cream cheese, softened and creamed*

2   *3½-ounce boxes instant vanilla pudding, prepared according to package instructions*

1   *16-ounce carton nondairy whipped topping*

1   *16-ounce can milk chocolate icing*

Layer one-fourth of the graham cracker crumbs in the bottom of a 9 x 13-inch pan. In a large bowl cream together the cream cheese, pudding, and whipped topping. Spread one-third of the cream cheese mixture on the graham crackers. Repeat the layers two more times, and then end with a layer of graham crackers. Spread the icing on top. Chill and serve.

SERVES 10 TO 12.

The Booth Brothers

The Booth Brothers are (left to right) father Ron and sons Ronnie and Michael.

Kathy's Chocolate Gravy

1   cup sugar

½   cup cocoa

2   tablespoons all-purpose flour

2   cups milk

2   tablespoons butter

In a skillet combine the sugar, cocoa, and flour. Blend in the milk. Bring to a boil and thicken to your liking. (You can add more or less milk.) Pour into a gravy bowl and add the butter. Mix until creamy. Serve with hot buttered biscuits.

MAKES 3 CUPS.

Kathy Watson

TOUCHING ALL THE BASSES

Match the Favorite Bass Singer with the year he was awarded that title by The Singing News Fan Awards:

1. Billy Todd
2. Paul Downing
3. Mike Holcomb
4. Buddy Liles
5. Ray Dean Reese
6. George Younce
7. Rex Nelon
8. Tim Riley

A. 1973
B. 1971, 1972
C. 1977
D. 1974, 1975, 1976, 1978
E. 1980, 1982
F. 1989, 1990, 1991
G. 1979, 1985
H. 1981, 1983, 1984, 1986, 1987, 1988, 1992, 1993, 1994, 1995, 1996

Answers
1. B, 2. A, 3. D, 4. C, 5. G, 6. H, 7. E, 8. F

Good Book Chocolate Goodie

½   cup (1 stick) margarine

1½   cups all-purpose flour

2   tablespoons sugar

1½   cups pecans

1   8-ounce container nondairy whipped topping

1   8-ounce package cream cheese, softened

1   cup confectioners' sugar

1   3½-ounce package instant vanilla pudding

1   3½-ounce package instant chocolate pudding

2¾   cups milk

     Shaved chocolate or chopped nuts

Preheat the oven to 350°. In a large bowl mix together the margarine, flour, sugar, and pecans. Spread into a 9 x 13-inch baking dish. Bake for 25 minutes. (Be careful: It burns easily.) Cool.

In a separate bowl cream together half of the whipped topping, the cream cheese, and the confectioners' sugar and spread over the cooled crust.

In a medium bowl combine the puddings and milk and beat until thick. Let cool in the refrigerator for about 5 minutes. Spread the pudding on top of the cream cheese mixture. Top with the remaining whipped topping and the shaved chocolate or nuts. Delicious!

SERVES 9 TO 12.

The Singing Halyards

LaBreeska's Delight

1¾   cups all-purpose flour

½   cup plus 6 tablespoons (1¾ sticks) margarine or butter, melted

1   cup chopped nuts

1   8-ounce package cream cheese

1¼   cups confectioners' sugar

1   cup nondairy whipped topping

1   3½-ounce package instant vanilla pudding mix

1   3½-ounce package instant chocolate pudding mix

3   cups milk

Preheat the oven to 350°. In a medium bowl mix the flour, margarine, and nuts. Pat into the bottom of a 9 x 13-inch baking dish. Bake for 25 minutes. Cool.

In a large bowl combine the cream cheese, confectioners' sugar, and whipped topping. Spread on the cooled crust. In separate bowls mix the chocolate pudding with half of the milk, and mix the vanilla pudding with the remaining milk. After each pudding has set, mix together gently and spread on top of the cream cheese layer. Chill. Cut into squares and serve.

SERVES 12.

LaBreeska and Joel Hemphill • The Hemphills

Joel and LaBreeska Hemphill have bunches of fun with the Fruit of the Loom fruits back stage at a 1996 taping for The Nashville Network's Prime Time Country.

Blueberry Icebox Cake

1½   cups graham cracker crumbs

½   cup confectioners' sugar

½   cup melted butter

4   eggs, well beaten

2   cups sugar

2   8-ounce packages cream cheese, softened

1   20-ounce can blueberry pie mix (with juice of ½ lemon added)

Nondairy whipped topping

Preheat the oven to 350°. Coat a 9 x 13-inch pan with nonstick cooking spray. In a medium bowl mix the graham cracker crumbs, confectioners' sugar, and butter together and pat the mixture into the pan to form a crust. In a large bowl blend the eggs, sugar, and cream cheese together with an electric mixer until smooth. Spread the mixture over the crumb mixture. Bake for about 30 minutes.

Pour the blueberry pie mix over top of the slightly cooled cake. Keep in the refrigerator until served. Top with the whipped topping.

SERVES 6 TO 8.

Cindy Larson • The Deweys

The Deweys of 1978. Left to right are Levoy, Cleon, Cindy, and Suzanne.

Angel Delight

2   3½-ounce packages instant vanilla pudding

4   cups milk

1   12-ounce carton nondairy whipped topping

1   large angel food cake, cut into small pieces or cubed

1   cup sour cream

1   21-ounce can cherry pie filling

In a large bowl mix together the instant pudding and milk. Fold half of the nondairy whipped topping into the pudding mixture. In a large dish make a layer using half of the cake pieces, then top with a layer of half of the pudding mixture. Spoon all of the cherry pie filling over the pudding mixture. Layer the remaining cake pieces over the cherry pie filling, and then the remaining pudding. Top with the remaining whipped topping. Refrigerate overnight.

SERVES 10.

Joyce Brown • The Browns

Thread of Hope Oreo Cookie Dessert

1   20-ounce package Oreos, crushed

¼   cup (½ stick) margarine, melted

1   8-ounce package cream cheese, softened

1   cup confectioners' sugar

2   6-ounce packages instant vanilla pudding

3½   cups milk

1   8-ounce carton nondairy whipped topping

Mix the Oreos and margarine together, reserving enough Oreo crumbs to sprinkle on top later. Press the mixture into a 9 x 13-inch pan to make a crust. In a mixing bowl combine the cream cheese and confectioners' sugar. Mix well and set aside. In a separate bowl mix together the pudding and milk. Combine the cream cheese and pudding mixtures and then fold in the whipped topping. Pour the mixture over the crust and sprinkle with the remaining Oreos.

SERVES 10 TO 12.

Jeff and Sheri Easter

Dirt Cake

¼   cup (½ stick) margarine

1   8-ounce package cream cheese

1   cup confectioners' sugar

2   6-ounce packages vanilla instant pudding

3½   cups milk

1   12-ounce carton nondairy whipped topping

1   20-ounce package Oreos

In a large bowl cream the margarine, cream cheese, and confectioners' sugar and set aside. In a separate bowl mix the pudding and milk together, and fold in the whipped topping. Combine with the cream cheese mixture. Crush the cookies in a blender. Layer the cookies and creamed mixture in a 10-inch plastic flower pot or ice cream bucket, ending with cookies.

SERVES 10 TO 12.

April Potter • Harper & Associates

April Potter of Harper & Associates holds a plaque commemorating the first Number One song by Brian Free and Assurance, "For God So Loved." Pictured with April are Brian Free and Assurance members (left to right) Randy Crawford, Bob Caldwell, Jon McBroom, and Brian Free.

Easy Banana Pudding

Vanilla wafers

6   to 8 ripe bananas

1   3½-ounce package instant vanilla pudding

2   cups milk

Nondairy whipped topping

Cocktail peanuts, crushed

Line a dish with vanilla wafers. Slice the bananas on top of the wafers. In a medium bowl combine the pudding mix and milk, and mix thoroughly. Pour the pudding mixture on top of the bananas, being sure to completely cover the bananas. Chill in the refrigerator until firm. Cover with the nondairy whipped topping and crushed peanuts.

SERVES 10.

Mary Tom Reid • The Speers

The Speer Family around 1936, back, left to right: Mom, Rosa Nell, Dad, and Brock; front, left to right: Mary Tom and Ben.

Test of Time Banana Pudding

1	6-ounce package instant vanilla pudding
3	cups milk
1	cup sour cream
1	16-ounce carton nondairy whipped topping
1	12-ounce box vanilla wafers
7	ripe bananas

In a medium bowl mix the pudding and milk until well blended and smooth. Fold in the sour cream. Fold in the whipped topping. In a large bowl layer the wafers, then bananas, and then pudding, until all is used. Sprinkle crushed vanilla wafers on top. Cover with plastic wrap and refrigerate.

SERVES 8 TO 10.

The Kingdom Heirs

Top Banana Pudding

1	14-ounce can sweetened condensed milk
1½	cups cold water
1	3½-ounce package instant vanilla pudding
2	cups nondairy whipped topping
	Vanilla wafers
	Sliced bananas

In a bowl combine the sweetened condensed milk and water. Beat in the pudding mix with an electric mixer. Chill for 5 minutes. Fold in the whipped topping. Layer the mixture into a bowl with layers of vanilla wafers and sliced bananas. End with the pudding mixture on top. Refrigerate until ready to serve.

SERVES 10.

Trish Holman • Homeland Records

The Love of Jesus Strawberry Pudding

1   quart washed and capped strawberries

1   6-ounce package strawberry gelatin

½   cup sugar

2   3½-ounce boxes instant vanilla pudding

3   cups milk

1   8-ounce carton sour cream

1   12-ounce carton nondairy whipped topping

1   12-ounce box vanilla wafers

In a saucepan combine the strawberries, gelatin, and sugar, and cook over medium heat until the gelatin and sugar melt. In a large bowl mix the pudding and milk. Add the sour cream and ¾ of the whipped topping. In a 9 x 13-inch dish make a layer of vanilla wafers, followed by the pudding mix and the strawberry mix. Repeat the layers. Top with the remaining whipped topping and garnish with a few strawberries.

SERVES 9.

Annie and Charles Johnson • Charles Johnson & the Revivers

Charles Johnson & The Revivers are one of the rare black groups in Southern Gospel. Among their hit songs are "The Love of Jesus "and "The Winds of This World." Johnson has been in music for thirty-five years and was previously in The Consolators, The Golden Gate Quartet, and The Sensational Nightingales. Left to right are Steve Boyd, Tracy Pierce, Maurice Morgan, Sr., Charles Johnson, and Joe Yancy.

O For A Thousand Rice Puddings

When I was a child, every week we would go to my grandmother's house for Sunday dinner. My grandmother always liked to make a big pudding. I would watch that rice pudding come out of the oven, and it always seemed like there was enough to feed the whole neighborhood! I have wonderful memories of those Sunday afternoons, and I still love rice pudding.

2	cups cooked rice
1	cup milk
¾	cup firmly packed brown sugar
3	eggs, lightly beaten
3	tablespoons melted butter or margarine
¾	cup raisins
½	teaspoon vanilla extract
	Dash grated nutmeg
1	cup whipped cream

Preheat the oven to 350°. In a 1-quart casserole or baking dish combine the rice, milk, brown sugar, eggs, and butter. Place the casserole in a baking pan. Fill the pan with a enough water to go halfway up the sides of the casserole dish. Bake for 30 minutes.

Remove the rice pudding from the oven. Stir in the raisins and vanilla. Sprinkle with nutmeg. Return to the oven. Bake for 30 minutes.

Serve hot or chilled, topped with whipped cream.

SERVES 6 TO 8.

Kelly Nelon Thompson • The Nelons

The Nelons

The Atlanta-based family group The Nelons has been at the forefront of Southern gospel for many years. Rex Nelon, patriarch of the group, has been in the business for more than forty years and sang for many years with The LeFevres. In the 1970s, The LeFevres sold the group to Nelon and he changed the name to The Rex Nelon Singers, later The Nelons.

The group consists of Rex, daughter Kelly Nelon Thompson, her husband Jerry Thompson, Atlantan Amy Roth, and bassist/vocalist Jason Clark.

The Nelons have won six Dove Awards, numerous *Singing News* Fan Awards, and a New York Film Festival Bronze Award. They been nominated for Grammys three times.

Among their many Top Ten hits are "No More Tears," "Bring My Children Home," "Come Morning, The Son's Coming Up," "We Will Wear a Robe and a Crown," "O for a Thousand Tongues," and "I'll Talk to the Father."

Kelly has also scored as a solo singer with her hits "He'll Go Out of His Way," "We Can't Waste Any Time," and "Don't Stop Praying for Me," her duet with Bruce Carroll.

The family harmony gets even more balance through the lyrics and music of Jerry, the principal songwriter of the group.

And then there's the family unit. "I always wanted to sing with family," says Rex Nelon, a native of Asheville, North Carolina. "Early in my career, I was away most of the time singing with different groups. Singing together with family has given us a chance to get some time back together."

"Being able to stand on stage and sing for Jesus, letting the whole world know what He means to us, is such a great honor," Kelly says. "I believe I was called, as was the whole group, to encourage people."

The Nelons of Atlanta, Georgia, ushered in the popularity of the family group in the modern era of Southern Gospel. Left to right are Kelly Nelon Thompson, Amy Roth, Rex Nelon, and Jerry Thompson.

Super Homemade Freezer Cream

2   14-ounce cans evaporated milk

2   cups sugar

1   tablespoon imitation vanilla flavoring

    Milk (2 percent)

In a 1-gallon metal ice cream freezer container mix the evaporated milk, sugar, and vanilla. Add milk to the fill line on a 1-gallon metal ice cream freezer container. Stir. Put in the paddle and top with the lid. Place the container in the freezer barrel. Put in a layer of crushed ice, then a layer of ice cream salt (and a little table salt), rotating until the ice is above the rim of the metal cream container. Cover with a towel and plug in the machine. When it begins to freeze, the machine will start to grind. Listen carefully. When the grinding stops, the ice cream is frozen. Turn off the machine immediately. Raise the bucket from the ice barrel and pour a small amount of clear water over the top to remove any salt from the lid. Enjoy.

    For other flavors, you can add a carton of thawed strawberries, 2 mashed bananas, or 4 fresh peaches (chopped and mashed). Just add the additional ingredients to the basic mixture and add the 2 percent milk last because you won't need as much.

MAKES 1 GALLON.

Jack Toney • The Statesmen

Saved to the Uttermost Ice Cream

2   cups sugar

4   eggs

1   14-ounce can sweetened condensed milk

1   12-ounce can evaporated milk

2   tablespoons vanilla extract

    Milk

In a bowl beat the sugar and eggs together. Add the sweetened condensed milk, evaporated milk, and vanilla extract. Pour into a 1-gallon ice cream freezer container. Add milk to fill to the fill line. Freeze as directed.

    Variation: Add 3 mashed bananas, 1 20-ounce can no-sugar-added crushed pineapple, 1 cup orange juice.

MAKES 1 GALLON.

Faye Speer • The Speers

Gold Bars Dessert

1   cup graham cracker crumbs

½   cup saltine cracker crumbs

3   Butterfinger candy bars, crushed

2   3½-ounce packages French vanilla instant pudding

2   cups milk

1   quart vanilla ice cream, softened

      Nondairy whipped topping

Preheat the oven to 375°. In a medium bowl combine the graham cracker crumbs, saltine cracker crumbs, and two of the Butterfinger candy bars. Press into a 9 x 13-inch baking pan. Bake for 12 to 15 minutes. Cool.

In a large bowl mix together the pudding, milk, and ice cream. Pour over the crust. Top with nondairy whipped topping and the remaining crumbled Butterfinger. Chill until time to serve.

SERVES 6 TO 8.

Adam Borden • Gold City Quartet

When My Knees Touch Gold Butter Pecan Ice Cream

1	cup pecans
2	tablespoons margarine
3	eggs
1	3-ounce package vanilla pudding
1½	cups sugar
	Milk
½	teaspoon maple flavoring
½	teaspoon butter flavoring
1	teaspoon vanilla extract
1	14-ounce can sweetened condensed milk
½	pint heavy cream

In a skillet slowly brown the pecans in the margarine. Set aside. In a heavy saucepan mix the eggs, vanilla pudding mix, sugar, and a small amount of milk. Cook slowly over low heat. Add the maple flavoring, butter flavoring, vanilla, sweetened condensed milk, heavy cream, and pecans. Pour the mixture into a 1-gallon ice cream freezer. Finish filling the freezer with milk. Freeze the cream according to the freezer directions.

MAKES 1 GALLON.

Lori Thornton

Anchormint Sauce for Ice Cream

1/3   cup light corn syrup

3   tablespoons crushed peppermint candy

1   tablespoon butter

1   cup marshmallow cream

1/4   cup evaporated milk

1/2   teaspoon vanilla extract

In a small saucepan combine the corn syrup, candy, and butter. Bring to a boil over medium heat. Stir occasionally. Boil for 5 minutes. Remove the pan from the heat. Blend in the marshmallow cream, evaporated milk, and vanilla. Serve over ice cream.

MAKES 1 CUP.

The Anchormen

The Anchormen, a group from Goldsboro, North Carolina, formed in 1979, and were among the first Christian artists to perform gospel music at country music's Fan Fair. Clockwise from top left are Ricky Wilhide, Dwayne West, Steve Ladd, Eddie Johnson, Jeff Chapman, and Chris Wood.

Bending Chestnut Dessert

1   large angel food cake, broken into pieces

6   Butterfinger candy bars, refrigerated and crushed

1   pint whipping cream, whipped

¼   cup butter

4   egg yolks

2   teaspoons vanilla extract

2   cups confectioners' sugar

In a mixing bowl whip together the butter, egg yolks, and vanilla. Add the confectioners' sugar and blend well. Fold the butter mixture into the whipped cream. In a 9 x 13 inch dish or a trifle bowl layer the cake, cream mixture, and candy. Repeat the layers. Refrigerate overnight.

SERVES 10 TO 12.

Beverly and Lynn Fox • The Fox Brothers

Cheery Cherry Yum Yum

1   small box vanilla wafers, crushed

½   cup (1 stick) butter

½   cup sugar

18   ounces cream cheese, softened

¾   cup sugar

1   teaspoon vanilla

2   envelopes Dream Whip

1   cup milk

1   21-ounce can cherry pie filling

In a medium bowl mix the crushed vanilla wafers and butter, and use half of the mixture to make a crust in a 9 x 13-inch pan. Mix together all of the remaining ingredients except the pie filling, and beat until stiff. Spread half of the cream mixture over the crust. Spread the pie filling over the mixture and then add the remaining cream mixture. Top with the remaining crumb mixture. Refrigerate.

SERVES 10 TO 12.

Debbie and Randy Fox • The Fox Brothers

Mother's Cookies

2	*cups (4 sticks) butter (do not substitute margarine)*
2	*cups sugar*
4	*cups all-purpose flour*

In a large bowl cream together the butter and sugar. Add the flour all at once and mix until well blended. Separate the dough into 4 equal parts. Roll the dough parts into rolls. Wrap in plastic wrap. Chill in the refrigerator or freezer until firm.

Slice the dough thinly. Place on a cookie sheet. Bake at 300° for 15 minutes. Cookies will be yellow; do not brown. Let the cookies stand on the cookie sheet for a few seconds to set. Remove to a paper towel to cool. The dough may be frozen unbaked and kept in the freezer for several weeks, if desired.

MAKES 8 DOZEN.

Candy Hemphill–Christmas

Candy Hemphill-Christmas is a solo performer who began her professional career at age thirteen as a member of the famed Hemphill family. One of her best known tunes is "Master of the Wind."

Sundays Sandies

But they're great for any day!

1	cup (2 sticks) butter or margarine
1/3	cup sugar
2	teaspoons water
2	tablespoons vanilla extract
2	cups sifted all-purpose flour
1	cup chopped pecans
	Confectioners' sugar

Preheat the oven to 325°. In a bowl cream the butter and sugar. Add the water and vanilla and mix well. Blend in the flour. Stir in the nuts. Shape into fingers and place on an ungreased cookie sheet. Bake until slightly brown. Roll in confectioners' sugar.

MAKES 3 TO 4 DOZEN.

The Dixie Echoes

Miraculous No Bake Oatmeal Cookies

2	cups sugar (firmly packed brown or white)
1/2	cup (1 stick) butter
1/2	cup cream
3	tablespoons cocoa
1/2	cup peanut butter
3	cups quick oatmeal
1	teaspoon vanilla extract

In a saucepan combine the sugar, butter, and cream, and bring to a rolling boil, stirring constantly. Remove the pan from the heat. Add the cocoa and peanut butter and stir until blended. Then add the oatmeal and vanilla, and stir. Drop by the teaspoonful onto waxed paper. You can add nuts or coconut if you wish.

MAKES ABOUT 3 DOZEN.

Merita Browder • The Browders

Peacemaking Peanut Butter Cookies

½	cup shortening
¾	cup peanut butter
½	cup sugar
½	cup firmly packed brown sugar
1	egg
½	teaspoon vanilla extract
1½	cups all-purpose flour
1	teaspoon soda
⅛	teaspoon salt

Preheat the oven to 350°. In a mixing bowl cream the shortening, peanut butter, and the sugars with an electric mixer. Add the egg and vanilla and blend well. Mix in the remaining ingredients. The batter will be stiff. Drop the batter by the spoonful onto a cookie sheet. Bake for 8 to 10 minutes. Do not overbake. Let cool for 5 minutes before removing from the cookie sheet.

MAKES 3 TO 4 DOZEN.

Steve Warren

J.D. Sumner and The Stamps of recent years have included, clockwise from bottom, J.D. Sumner, Steve Warren, Ed Enoch, Ed Hill, and C.J. Amalgren. Steve currently is a backup singer for Wayne Newton.

Great Smoky Mountain Smackers

1   20-ounce roll refrigerator chocolate chip cookie dough
36   chocolate kisses, unwrapped
     All-purpose flour

Preheat the oven to 350°. Cut the dough into 9 slices. Cut each circle into 4 pieces. Lightly grease 3 miniature muffin tins (12 cups per tin). Place 1 piece of dough into each cup. With a pinch of flour on your finger tips, form the dough into cups. Place a chocolate kiss in the center of each cup. Bake for 10 to 12 minutes. Let the cookies cool in the pan for 15 minutes before removing to a cooling rack.

MAKES 3 DOZEN COOKIES.
The Kingdom Heirs

Good Show Lemon Butter Snowbars

Crust:
½   cup (1 stick) butter, softened
1⅓   cups all-purpose flour
¼   cup sugar

Filling:
2   eggs
¾   cup sugar
2   tablespoons baking powder
3   tablespoons lemon juice
     Confectioners' sugar

Preheat the oven to 350°. In a 1½-quart mixing bowl combine the crust ingredients. Mix on low speed about 1 minute until blended. Pat into an ungreased 8-inch square baking pan. Bake near the center of the oven for 15 to 20 minutes or until the crust is brown on the edges.

    Meanwhile, prepare the filling. In a medium bowl mix the eggs, ¾ cup of sugar, baking powder, and lemon juice. Pour the filling over the partially baked crust. Return to the oven for 18 to 20 minutes or until set. Sprinkle with confectioners' sugar. Allow to cool and then serve.

SERVES 6.
The Easter Brothers

Agape Love Brownies

½   cup (1 stick) plus 5 tablespoons margarine

½   cup cocoa

1⅓   cups all-purpose flour

1   teaspoon baking powder

½   teaspoon salt

2   cups sugar

4   eggs

2   teaspoons vanilla extract

1   cup pecans (optional)

Chocolate Icing:

¼   cup (½ stick) butter

2   to 3 tablespoons cocoa.

2   to 3 cups confectioners' sugar

¼   cup milk.

Preheat the oven to 350°. In a saucepan over low heat melt the margarine. Stir in ½ cup of cocoa until dissolved. In a large bowl mix the flour, baking powder, salt, and sugar. Cream the eggs with the dry ingredients. Pour the cocoa mixture over the flour mixture and mix well. Add the vanilla and pecans. Pour the batter into a greased 9 x 13-inch pan. Bake for 35 to 40 minutes.

In a saucepan melt the butter and stir in 2 to 3 tablespoons of cocoa until dissolved. Remove from heat add the confectioners' sugar and milk. Mix until creamy and spread onto warm brownies. Enjoy!

MAKES 12 GOOD-SIZED BROWNIES.

Linda Reeves

Sunday Date Balls

Cindy says Archie has a lot of favorites, but these were his pick to share with you.

1   *cup (2 sticks) margarine*

1   *cup sugar*

1   *8-ounce package dates, chopped*

1   *cup chopped nuts*

2   *cups Rice Krispies*

1   *teaspoon vanilla extract*

       Confectioners' sugar

In a saucepan combine the margarine, sugar, and dates, and cook over medium heat, stirring constantly. Remove the pan from the heat and add the nuts, Rice Krispies, and vanilla. Let cool. Shape into 1- to 2-inch balls and place on waxed paper. Sprinkle lightly with confectioners' sugar. These keep nicely in an airtight container.

MAKES ABOUT 3 DOZEN.

Cindy and Archie Watkins • The Inspirations

The Inspirations are, clockwise from far left, bass guitarist Myron Cook, bass singer Mike Holcomb, lead singer Troy Burns, manager-pianist Martin Cook, baritone Eddie Dietz, and tenor Archie Watkins. They kicked off their career in the spring of 1964 at Swain County High School in Bryson City, North Carolina, and have since gone on to win The Singing News award as top gospel group six times. Gospel music-loving fans know the group best for its "Singing in the Smokies" event held from June to October at Inspiration Park in Bryson City. It is one of the most famous family-oriented music festivals in the world.

Thank You Lord Fried Apple Pies

When making pies using store-bought pie crusts, be sure you can see well. The following story is from our secretary, Marian.

Just before Thanksgiving and expecting company, I made my special homemade pumpkin pies with store-bought crusts. My company was especially fond of my pumpkin pies. I had wrapped them in cellophane and put them in the fridge. Just before dinner, I took them out of the fridge and was in for a shock. The pies that I had taken from the oven were flat. One of my guests said, "That's O.K. We'll eat them," and he started to cut the pies. "What did you put in these pies, cement? They won't slice!" And with that he pulled out the paper liners that are always in frozen store-bought crusts. Everybody had a good laugh. Now when I'm trying to put one over, I always check to see if the paper liners are thrown away, but not with the pie. By the way, one of my guests is now with a major gospel singing group. Thanks, Roger!

Filling:

> *A good thick applesauce sweetened to taste. (You can substitute any fruit filling that you like.)*

Pastry:

2   *cups all-purpose flour*

1   *teaspoon baking powder*

1   *teaspoon salt*

½   *cup (1 stick) margarine (mash with fork and cut into dry ingredients)*

8   *to 10 tablespoons milk*

Mix well and make into 10 balls for pies. Roll out the balls, add some filling, fold the pastry over and crimp the edges. Poke a few holes in the pastry with a fork to vent steam. Fry the pies 1 at a time in hot oil.

MAKES 10 PIES.

Eddie Deitz • The Inspirations

Rosie's Fried Apple Pies

1   6-ounce package dried apples
1   8-count can refrigerator biscuits
     Vegetable oil

Cook the dried apples according to the package instructions, and allow to cool. Roll out the biscuits to form an extremely thin dough. Use a small saucer to cut the dough. Place a small amount of the cooled apples on one half of each piece of cut dough. Fold the dough over and crimp the edges together. With a fork, punch holes in the pie to let steam escape. Fry in vegetable oil over medium heat until brown on both sides. Good luck!

MAKES ABOUT A DOZEN.
Rosa Nell Speer Powell • The Speers

The Speer Family entertains thousands of fans at an outdoor festival in the 1970s.

Get the Rhythm Chocolate Fried Pies

	Enough pie dough for 2 9-inch pie crusts
8	level teaspoons cocoa
8	heaping tablespoons sugar
	Pinch salt
½	teaspoon ground cinnamon
	Butter
1	teaspoon vanilla extract
	Shortening for frying

Prepare the pie dough according to the recipe directions and knead until firm. Divide the dough into quarters. Mix the cocoa, sugar, salt, and cinnamon and divide into fourths.

Roll a piece of the dough into a circle measuring about 6 inches in diameter. Smooth one-fourth of the cocoa mixture over half of the crust. Place 4 thin slices of butter over the cocoa mixture and then sprinkle ¼ teaspoon of vanilla over the mixture. Fold the crust into a half moon and seal the edges with a fork. Fry in a non-stick skillet in ¼ inch of shortening. Turn when brown. Repeat with the remaining dough and cocoa mixture to make 4 pies.

MAKES 4 PIES.

Carroll Rawlings • The Rhythm Masters

Lou's Cheesy Apples

8	Granny Smith apples
¾	cup (1½ sticks) butter or margarine, softened
½	pound Velveeta cheese, cut into small cubes
1½	cups sugar
1¼	cups self-rising flour

Preheat the oven to 350°. Peel and thinly slice the apples. In a saucepan cook the apples with in a little water until barely tender. Drain, and then layer the apples into a 9 x 13-inch baking dish. In a separate bowl mix the remaining ingredients. Spread the mixture over top of the apples. Bake for 25 minutes.

SERVES 10 TO 12.

Trish Holman • Homeland Records

I'm Gonna Shout All Over Heaven Sugarless Apple Pie

1   6-ounce can frozen apple juice (no sugar added)

2   tablespoons all-purpose flour

1   teaspoon ground cinnamon

$\frac{1}{2}$ teaspoon salt

5   to 6 red delicious apples, peeled and sliced

2   tablespoons margarine

        Nutmeg

2   9-inch pie shells

Preheat the oven to 350°. In a saucepan heat the apple juice over medium heat. In a small bowl mix the flour, cinnamon, and salt, and add to the juice. Cook until thick, stirring frequently. Coat the apple slices with the juice mixture. Fill 1 of the pie crusts with the apples. Dot with margarine. Place the other crust over the apples and sprinkle with nutmeg. Bake for 50 to 55 minutes.

SERVES 6.

Haskell Cooley • The Cooleys

Candy Capers

We tried to develop in our children the idea that candy wasn't good for them. We thought if we started teaching them this early in their childhood and not encouraging them to eat candy, they wouldn't develop a taste for it. This approach worked very well for our son, Cason, who is now eighteen. He doesn't eat very much candy. It didn't work for our daughter, Camissa, who is now twelve. She loves candy!

One night we were singing at Barton's Tabernacle in Gilmer, Texas, with some other groups. Cason was three years old. When it came our turn to sing, the lady running the concession stand volunteered to watch Cason while we sang. When we finished singing and got Cason, the lady jokingly said, "Take this child away from here. He's making me lose business." When people asked for candy, Cason would tell them they shouldn't buy it because it was bad for them.

When Camissa was very small, she would have to sit with someone in the audience while we sang. We'd tell her not to ask for candy and gum. As we were singing, we'd notice her chewing on something. What she was doing was asking the people for candy or gum. If they didn't have any, they'd pass her on to someone else to see if they had any.

Haskell Cooley • The Cooleys

Cooley Cobbler

It's sugar free.

3	tablespoons cornstarch
1	12-ounce can frozen unsweetened apple juice concentrate
2	16-ounce cans sliced peaches, drained, or 4 cups fresh peaches
1	cup all-purpose flour
1½	teaspoons baking powder
3	tablespoons vegetable oil or melted margarine

Preheat the oven to 350°. In a saucepan mix the cornstarch with 1 cup of the juice concentrate. Heat until thick. Add the peaches, and stir until all are coated. Pour the mixture into an 9 x 13-inch casserole dish. In a small bowl stir together the flour and baking powder. Add the vegetable oil or margarine and remaining ½ cup of the juice concentrate to the flour mixture. Stir well. Drop the batter by spoonfuls onto the fruit mixture. Bake for 45 minutes or until the dough is cooked all the way through.

SERVES 6 TO 8.

Haskell Cooley and Family • The Cooleys

SOUTHERN GOSPEL PUBLICATIONS

The Gospel Voice, 515 Two Mile Parkway, Suite 212, Goodlettsville, TN 37072-2025

The Singing News, P.O. Box 2810, 330 University Hall Drive, Boone, NC 28607

Southern Gospel Source, P.O. Box 310, Beech Grove, Ind. 46107; 5235 Elmwood Ave., Suite B, Indianapolis, IN 46203

Southern Notes, 10891 Hwy. 79, Scottsboro, AL 35768

Trade Review, P.O. Box 2810, Boone, NC 28607

U.S. Gospel News, 603-B W. Matthews, Jonesboro, AR 72401

Easy Peachy Cream Cheese Dessert

¾	cup all-purpose flour
1	teaspoon baking powder
½	teaspoon salt
1	3¼-ounce package vanilla pudding and pie filling mix (not instant)
3	tablespoons butter
1	egg
½	cup milk
1	16-ounce can sliced peaches, reserving the juice
1	8-ounce package cream cheese
½	cup sugar
1	tablespoon sugar
½	teaspoon ground cinnamon

Preheat the oven to 350°. In a large bowl beat the flour, baking powder, salt, vanilla pudding, butter, egg, and milk with a mixer on medium speed, for 2 minutes. Pour into a 9-inch greased pie pan. Cover with the sliced peaches, leaving a 1-inch edge around the pan.

In a medium bowl mix together the cream cheese, 3 tablespoons of the reserved peach juice, and ½ cup of sugar. Spread over the peaches. Mix together 1 tablespoon of sugar and ½ teaspoon of cinnamon and sprinkle the mixture over the top of the pie. Bake at 350° for 30 to 35 minutes. For a 9 x 13-inch pan, double the recipe.

SERVES 6 TO 8.

Linda Reeves

Let the Hallelujahs Roll Pecan Pralines

When I lived in Louisiana, we called these "prawleens." In Tennessee, where I live now, they are called "prayleens." Any way you want to pronounce them, they are delicious!

1	*cup sugar*
1	*cup firmly packed dark brown sugar*
1	*tablespoon butter (salted)*
3	*tablespoons dark corn syrup*
5	*tablespoons water*
1	*teaspoon vanilla extract*
2	*cups pecan halves*

In a saucepan mix all the ingredients, except the pecans, together and bring to a boil. Add 2 cups of pecan halves. Stir and bring to a soft boil. Simmer for about 8 to 10 minutes. Remove the pan from the heat and stir until the mixture begins to lose its glossiness and the syrup thickens. Drop by the teaspoonful on waxed paper to cool. When cool, remove and store in an airtight container.

MAKES ABOUT 3 DOZEN.

John Starnes

Among the particpants at the 1996 Stellar Awards were, left to right, John Starnes, Lisa Daggs, Vestal Goodman, Beau Williams, and Jacky Jack White.

Jasmine's Christmas Fudge

1   20-ounce package almond bark

1   cup crunchy peanut butter

1   cup chopped pecans

Melt the almond bark in the microwave according to the package directions. Add the peanut butter and pecans. Mix well. Pour into a pan lined with waxed paper. Refrigerate until hard.

MAKES 1 ½ POUNDS.

Jasmine Christmas

Jasmine Christmas, nine-year-old daughter of evangelist Kent Christmas and Candy Hemphill-Christmas, sings on stage during her mother's concerts and also joins her grandparents Joel and LaBreeska Hemphill for a song or two on occasional tour dates.

Fabulous Peanut Butter Fudge

Peanut butter fudge at the Crabb house will be as certain as wrapping paper, Christmas trees, and ho-ho-ho come December. I found my mom's recipe when I was sixteen or so, and I have not missed a Christmas preparing and sharing my favorite candy. This is the first real dessert I learned to prepare, and I stick with the same recipe.

3	cups sugar
⅔	cup evaporated milk
¾	cup (1½ sticks) butter
7	ounces marshmallow cream
1	teaspoon vanilla extract
½	to ¾ cup peanut butter

Grease a 9 x 13-inch pan with butter. In a saucepan bring the sugar, milk, and butter to a boil over medium heat. Boil for 5 minutes, stirring constantly. After 5 minutes, remove the pan from the heat and add the marshmallow cream, vanilla, and peanut butter. Pour the mixture into the prepared pan. Cool and then cut into squares.

MAKES ABOUT 2½ TO 3 POUNDS.

Kathy Crabb • The Crabb Family

The Singing News

Southern Gospel's first successful magazine, *The Singing News*, was founded in 1969 in Pensacola, Florida, by J.G. Whitfield, a singer, quartet manager, and one of the business's hardest working promoters.

The idea came to Whitfield because of his admiration for J.D. Sumner's newsletter, *Good News*, but Whitfield realized that fans of Southern Gospel were hungering for something with a little more news and depth.

At the time Whitfield was already mailing out fliers to promote his concerts in the areas where his events would be taking place, so he had an extensive mailing list and was pretty sure he could gain access to the mailing list of several other promoters.

So, with Jerry Kirksey, who began his career in the field in 1960 working radio promotions for The Florida Boys, Whitfield set his idea in motion. Kirksey, as editor, hired Janice Cain to write and got some advice from a friend at the Pensacola newspaper. In May 1969, the first issue of *The Singing News*, in tabloid newspaper style, was mailed out to ninety thousand fans.

"*The Singing News* was a publication about singing. We were not in the subscription or advertising business," recalled Kirksey. "We just mailed it out for free."

As more and more promoters shared their mailing lists, *The Singing News*, indeed, became the word on what was coming and going on nationwide in Southern Gospel.

"Marvin Norcross, president of Canaan Records, said, 'I want to buy an ad.' So we really got into the publication business by accident," Kirksey said. "One thing led to another. It really didn't change and was still basically an instrument for promoting concerts, until Maurice Templeton came to me, and said 'let's put together a deal.'"

Templeton, a businessman who charters Holy Land tours and cruise ships for quartet-loving fans,

J.G. Whitfield was one of Southern Gospel's great promoters and conceived of the idea of a national gospel magazine which begot The Singing News in 1969.

brainstormed with Kirksey and the two purchased *The Singing News* in 1986 and converted it from a free publication to subscription.

At the time *The Singing News* had a mailing list of over 300,000 concert fans. Templeton and editor Kirksey converted the freebie paper into a slick-stock magazine and began selling subscriptions and ads.

Today, *The Singing News*, based in Boone, North Carolina, has a circulation base of 185,000 subscribers and is distributed nationally by Ingram. The monthly publication averages about 124 pages and is considered one of the top magazines in its field, with editor Kirksey the dean of Southern Gospel journalists.

⚜ARTIST INDEX⚛

RECIPE INDEX